TRAVELS OF A
TEA-TASTER'S DOG

Travels of a Tea-Taster's Dog

by

JENNY PIERSON

The Memoir Club

© Jenny Pierson 2000

First published in 2000 by
The Memoir Club
Whitworth Hall
Spennymoor
County Durham

British Library Cataloguing in
Publication Data.
A catalogue record for this book
is available from the
British Library.

ISBN: 1 84104 019-3

Typeset by George Wishart & Associates, Whitley Bay.
Printed by Bookcraft (Bath) Ltd.

Dedicated to all my family and to the six dogs we have had in our married life — but really to Leslie because without him, none of it would ever have happened!

Remembering 44 years of friendship with Margaret Holland, the world's greatest giggler, who died just before this book was published.

Contents

List of Illustrations ix

Letter from My Mother xi

Introduction xiii

Chapter 1   How it all began – teacher training and X-rays –
and a wedding 1

Chapter 2   Chittagong, 1955; enter Skipper and
we move to Calcutta 8

Chapter 3   1956 – Four months in Cochin and visits to Ooty . . 21

Chapter 4   Cochin ducks, U.K. leave and Calcutta pregnancy . . . 32

Chapter 5   The wedding that wasn't and problems
with a new posting 42

Chapter 6   Now we are four! 49

Chapter 7   U.K. leave in '59 and we try our hand
at amateur dramatics 55

Chapter 8   Holidays, hens and pups 68

Chapter 9   Arab horses, more plays and more pups! 80

Chapter 10   Trouble on S.S. *Canberra*. Skip becomes an actress . . . 86

Chapter 11   Much travelling and lots of disasters.
My radio career begins 93

Chapter 12   1965. Farewell, Colombo. Hello, Ireland,
Jambo, Nairobi! 103

Chapter 13   Our 'pleasure life' in Nairobi 114

Chapter 14   A shaggy dog show, television and bad news 127

Chapter 15   The case of the dog that barked in the night 137

Chapter 16   The Agricultural Show and the Safari Rally 144

Chapter 17   Safaris to Naivasha and Amboseli 151

Chapter 18   A win for Skip and illness 157

Chapter 19   Surgery for me, Skipper and the cat! 162

Chapter 20   The move to Mombasa and the coming of Mousie . . 168

Chapter 21   Thirty-one years later 182

List of Illustrations

This is how x-rays were developed in 1953! Dark room
technician Miss Circuitt hard at work for the osteopaths
in Dorset Square, London   2

The Tea-taster. Leslie in 1954, shortly after we met   5

Leslie before we got married, up in the Chittagong Hill Tracts,
1954   5

Our wedding day, April 16th, 1955 at St Mary's Church,
Beaconsfield. Leslie's mother, Netta, on left. My parents
on right, my favourite picture of them   6

Our first home, No.1 Amina Manzil in 1955. We had the flat
on the left, ground floor   9

Making soup on safari in the Chittagong Hill Tracts, 1955 11

Myself with Skipper on the veranda the day we got her.
Chittagong, 1955 13

Skip in Calcutta, November, 1955. She always had the
crooked paw 16

In Auckland Square, Calcutta, 1955 17

1956. The house in Cochin, then the only one owned
by Lipton's 24

Wenlock Downs, Ooty, 1956 27

Lipton Office bids us farewell on leaving Cochin in 1956 29

Skip staying with David and Sheila Marsh while we were
on leave 34

Skip with Neal, two months old, in Calcutta, 1957 45

'Shangri La', Colombo, 1959 50

John the cook with Neal, Joslin the ayah with Sarah
at Shangri La, 1959 50

Sevenoaks, 1959. Ma, Leslie, Alastair, with Geoff, Ann with
    Manda, and myself with Neal   57

Myself as the Vicar's wife, Leslie as the Bishop, Barry Whittington
    as an impostor vicar in *See How They Run*, Colombo, 1959 . . .   62

Neal, Sarah, Skip and prostrate mother Ping with her puppies,
    Colombo, January, 1963   78

At the Park Hill Hotel. Chris and Ann   87

Tess in the garden of the McMillan Road house in Nairobi, 1966 . 115

Tess keeps a safe distance while Sarah pats Rufus the rhino,
    an orphan at Tsavo, 1966 155

Stan Holland took this of Ping at the Shaggy Dog Show,
    Nairobi, 1967 158

Cup and rosette for Best in Show, Nairobi Shaggy Dog Show,
    1967 159

Our bungalow, Nyali, Mombasa, 1968 173

Lesley Holland having her hair done by Mousie, Mombasa, 1969 . 176

Sarah, Neal and Tess, Puttenham, 2000, our 45th Wedding
    Anniversary 183

**Letter from my mother, written in September, 1956,
as we were leaving the U.K. at the end of our first leave**

My dear Jenny and Leslie,

So much I want to say and the words don't come easily. It's really only to convey to you both, somehow, what happiness you have brought with you to us all these few weeks and to say what you know already, how close you always feel whether you are here or far away. Bless you for all your thoughtfulness and the way you have delighted us with the photographs. Lovely to have them and I hope they are just as successful when taken under tropical skies!

I hug you both and know as long as you have one another, you will be happy wherever you live.

Fondest love,

M

Introduction
(written in 1967)

A Warning, and an Explanation

THIS IS YET ANOTHER book about animals.

To be more specific, it is the story of a small mongrel bitch we acquired in East Pakistan, and of her subsequent travels and adventures with us during 14 years in India, Ceylon and Kenya. For those readers who are not so doggy-minded, it is also the story of the life of a tea-taster and his family abroad.

I offer no excuse for adding to the already vast amount of animal literature, except that I do feel that many animal stories, dog stories especially, fall either into the heartily technical variety, ('You will probably find your bitch will stand for the dog on the 12th to the 14th day') or else tend to be rather whimsical, with the dog only slightly less human than the author ('his dancing brown eyes said to me eagerly, "I want to go walkies, Missus"'), which I find a bit sick-making.

Of course, every dog-owner feels THEIR dog is the cleverest and most unique member of the dog world, which is very proper; I feel this way about Skipper, who is the heroine of this story. She has a vast advantage over some in being a mongrel, and therefore pretty unique in her looks. I have only once ever seen a dog that resembled her somewhat, and that was in Calcutta, at a time when I happened to be searching for a husband for Skip. I suddenly saw a woman with a black and white hairy dog waiting at the vet's. She was most startled when I cantered up to her all agog and gasped: 'Is yours a dog or a bitch? I'm looking for a husband!' She replied rather frigidly it was a bitch, so we parted with a few lame explanations from me and an amazed stare from her and her dog. Apparently the best marriages in dogdom are not handled in this haphazard fashion, and I was not much more successful in my next attempt to find Skip a husband, but more of that later.

When I was looking up my old diaries to refresh my memory, I started reading bits aloud to my husband, and at the end of an especially gruelling account of three months of ups and downs in Ceylon, we came to the conclusion that we have packed quite a bit of experiences into our twelve years together. Most of them have been shared by Skipper, who has covered 6,400 miles with us by air, sea, rail and road, and has helped us to rear three children — all, mercifully, as keen on animals as I am!

This, then, is what this book is about. I shall try very hard NOT to invest the animals in it with human feelings they don't possess, and I shall not make them 'talk'. I do, however, admit to blush-making private conversations with quite a few creatures, not just dogs, but hens, hamsters, guinea-pigs and horses, and I am not ashamed of being the kind of person who stops the car in order to rescue a death-defying hedgehog or chameleon who is trying to cross the road. The satisfaction I get from my good deed more than makes up for the amused stares and incredulity of passers-by.

P.S. Do remember that the following narrative was written 31 years ago! Ceylon is now Sri Lanka and Chittagong is now in Bangladesh, not East Pakistan.

CHAPTER 1

How it all began – teacher training
and x-rays – and a wedding

I FIND IT RATHER DIFFICULT to know exactly where to start, but as we would never have met Skipper if I hadn't been in Pakistan, it might be better to start with events that led to my going out East.

It all began with a phone call. I was living with a cousin and her family in London and working as receptionist and dark-room technician in the X-ray Department of the Osteopathic Clinic in Dorset Square. Before this, I had led a rather undecided existence. I left boarding school in 1949, determined to be a teacher. At one stage I had wanted to be a vet but finally decided there was too much book-work, and anyhow I hated hurting anything and would probably pass out if there was too much blood about. After much thought, I decided on teaching, mainly because of the holidays, which seemed a wonderful prospect. Since then my teaching friends have disillusioned me on this score! Anyhow, my teaching ambitions were much encouraged by an incident one Christmas Term. As I was tall and the eldest in the school, I was chosen to be Father Christmas for a party of local children from a nearby orphanage. I am always a sentimentalist, being the sort who is never dry-eyed for the first verse, even, of 'Abide With Me', and I was most touched at the way the children responded as I distributed my gifts. I was resplendent in red school cloak edged with cotton wool, beard and gumboots, and enjoying my cornucopian role immensely, especially when a small recipient piped: 'Can I kiss yer!' As I bent down, I thought to myself, 'This is what I want to do; I will mould the infant minds, make good citizens of them. They will return to me when I am old to thank me and I shall still have the holidays for animals. After all, children and animals have quite a lot in common sometimes.'

However, two crowded years later saw me bidding a regretful farewell to Miss Jebb, the Principal of the Froebel College at Roehampton; we had both decided that it wasn't, after all, quite the

1

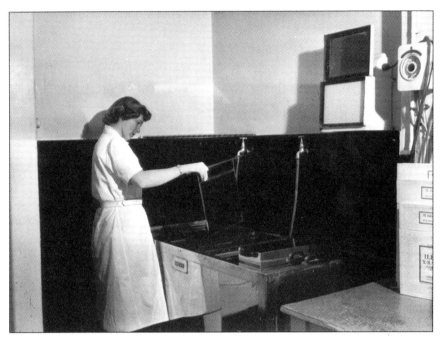

This is how x-rays were developed in 1953! Dark room technician Miss Circuitt hard at work for the osteopaths in Dorset Square, London.

career I was looking forward to. I, for one, found that to be a teacher, you didn't just sit and tell stories to the kiddies all day, or even just make them add, subtract and multiply. It all had to be done much more subtly. They had to Learn by Experience, more or less without knowing they were. This meant vast thought and planning by the teacher and much spare time spent making apparatus. Then one had to write lots of notes about how well one's ideas had worked out, and, in the last year of one's training, do a thesis on one particular child. This was a frightful chore and also my music wasn't up to much and my supervisor always turned up at the worst moments of chaos, when I was struggling to get all the little dears to be Great Big Policemen (much crashing in the bass with left hand) or, alternatively, 'Now let's all be tiny little fairies, EVER SO QUIET', ('No, Jimmy, you can't be excused now, dear'). On one historic occasion during a teaching practice, I lost a child. It was in my third year, and I was expected to be in charge of the class all on my own (it must have been frightful for the real teacher).

One five-year old was my special despair and delight. He was a blue-eyed, curly-haired Cockney called Arthur. One day he ran off after one of my catastrophic P.T. lessons outside, and of course my supervisor turned up like Banquo's ghost in a long green coat, in time to Hear All. The police were informed 'Just in case', so the class teacher told me serenely, as she carried on doling out the stew. Mercifully he was found in a butcher's shop nearby, but even so this incident was not forgotten by Authority, and it was read out like an indictment in my last interview with the Principal. (She did try to soften the blow a fraction by telling me kindly I had a nice manner with the children but it didn't alter the consequent ending of my Froebel career.)

Arthur also had me on the hop on another occasion. Just opposite the school was a small, typically soot-and-sparrow small London Park. We used to take the kids in sometimes for a change, and one day as the chattering crocodile meandered along, Arthur, bless him, said to me 'I'm goin' in 'ere' and darted into an ivy-camouflaged Gents that crouched nearby. This left me standing outside, my crocodile vanishing into the distance, hissing: 'Arthur, come out AT ONCE!' It earned me some pretty odd looks from a departing Gent before Arthur finally emerged. He eventually got t.b., and I heard they had to tie him to his bed to keep him from running about the ward, which sounds pretty typical.

Anyhow, as I was saying, Froebel and I parted regretfully, for I had had the most marvellous two years as a carefree student, and my parents, bless them, were very understanding and said I must have learnt SOMETHING in the two years, which of course I had. No one who has danced a Conga round the Albert Hall, or been to a hop at the Imperial College, or seen Piccadilly on Guy Fawkes night – no one, I repeat, can learn nothing from such experiences! Seriously, though, it was a wonderful time of companionship, of Nescafé round the gas fire, despair at coming exams, exhilaration at the latest boy friend, cream buns between lectures, and listening to Mrs Dale. However it hardly equipped me for earning my living and I finally decided to have a go at Domestic Science at Queen's College in Harley Street. The alternative was a Secretarial Course there, and I couldn't honestly see myself as the indispensable Miss Circuitt, all among files and typewriters, so I chose Domestic Science. I spent a happy year there, learning how to cook, sew and clean a house, and by a startling fluke, passed the exams with a first class certificate.

By now, I was 21 and so desperate to earn my own living, I used to darn my father's and brother's socks at 6d a hole. Just before I finished at Queen's, we heard that a good friend of Mummy's who was a radiographer at an osteopathic clinic, needed an assistant, and after a short interview, I got the job. My first monthly pay cheque, all £10 of it, was almost framed, but I needed the money.

All this past history finally brings us to May, 1954 and the phone-call. It was from a friend of a Fleet Air Arm acquaintance of mine. Mrs Bishop, who was the kindest soul on earth, said that a woman doctor friend of hers had a brother in Lipton's Tea who was on leave for four months from Pakistan. He didn't know many people, and could I come along to the Haverstock Arms some time and meet him? Funnily enough, I wasn't that keen. I was busy at work partially undressing all stratas of society from the aristocracy to the humblest citizens (if you have never asked Lord Montgomery to undress down to his long woolly pants, you have never really LIVED). My spare time was taken up with art classes, Civil Defence lectures in First Aid, rushing about on emergency calls in ambulances, helping in the canteen of a boys' club or helping the Fleet Air Arm to pass its leave happily.

I regret to say that the scales were tipped in favour of this unknown tea-taster from Pakistan by Mrs Bishop; with her usual low cunning, she informed me that he had a brand new car. He could probably take me home in time for my art class or whatever it was I had on the day she had fixed. Now I was used to the penniless student, 'let's-go-Dutch' sort of boyfriend, and very occasionally one would borrow Dad's jalopy – but someone with a new car...! That did it, and it seems an odd reflection on Life that this mercenary attitude eventually won me a jolly good husband; it doesn't seem right, somehow, but that's how it was. (It was a lovely car, a glossy black Zephyr, and even had a wireless.)

One thing led to another and three months later, Leslie and I were engaged. He did the thing properly, and came to the flat to ask my parents formally for my hand in marriage, and I have seldom spent such a nerve-wracking half hour waiting for him to arrive. I even took my pulse, which was hammering away, I discovered, at 110 a minute! At last the Zephyr swept round the corner of Prince Albert Road, and soon we were all sipping tea, both of us wondering how on earth to begin. I'd never really considered before, but a man can't just suddenly

The Tea-taster. Leslie in 1954, shortly after we met.

Leslie before we got married, up in the Chittagong Hill Tracts, 1954.

Our wedding day, April 16th, 1955 at St. Mary's Church, Beaconsfield. Leslie's mother, Netta, on left. My parents on right, my favourite picture of them.

lay down his teacup in cold blood and say to his girlfriend's parents that he'd like to marry her. We sat and sat and I began to get the giggles. Mummy thought we were behaving a bit oddly and finally, asked what was going on and it all came out. Poppa turned up his hearing aid in a rush, and we hurried through the remains of tea and then went up to my uncle's pub nearby to open a bottle of bubbly!

Leslie went back to Pakistan for eight months and returned the following April for a fortnight. We crammed in visits to Moss Bros, the vicar, various relatives, a party, the wedding, the honeymoon and a visit to the office – all into those two weeks, so it was almost a relief to clamber into an Argonaut at London Airport and set off to Karachi.

CHAPTER 2

Chittagong, 1955; enter Skipper
and we move to Calcutta

WE SPENT FIVE HOT DAYS IN Karachi, staying at the imposing Palace Hotel. The management knew Leslie was newly married, and on our arrival we were conducted to a huge apartment shaped like a medieval tower, and I was given a vast, very rich cake. We couldn't possibly finish it in five days, so I used to feed it guiltily to the dozens of crows and kites that were outside, throwing up chunks for them out of the window. Outside, I could see the large square where the old Aga Khan was weighed in gold (or was it diamonds?) – anyhow it sounded very imposing. It was the time of Ramadan, the Muslim festival in which, during the hours of daylight, no devout Muslim will eat or drink – in that heat a terrible trial. The office used to start very early, about seven o'clock, and finish at lunchtime for the day. This was nice for me as Leslie used to drive me to the beach not far off, and we had some wonderful swims. In the mornings I used to potter about and daringly go for short walks, for I was petrified with fear of getting lost. I was also asked out to coffee by the Tea Department Manager's wife, and started badly by tripping over the mat as I went in at the front door; it was opened by an imposing gentleman in white. He was wearing a huge turban with a sort of fan on it and a great wide belt round the waist of a snow white jacket. No wonder I didn't look where I put my feet!

Five days later we left Karachi. I was glad we weren't actually living there, it was so hot and dusty and everywhere was covered in a film of red grit. Furthermore, I wasn't keen on the glimpses one had of the overloaded donkeys and emaciated pi-dogs. The camels fascinated me; they were so aloof and snooty and seemed in better heart than the other animals. I knew when I came to the East that I would suffer agonies at the suffering of animals and birds there and although well meaning folk tried to tell me I'd soon get used to it, I never have, and I'd be ashamed if I did fail to pity some wretched, badly treated beast just because I'd seen it all before.

*Our first home, No. 1 Amina Manzil in 1955. We had the
flat on the left, ground floor.*

We arrived at the little airport at Chittagong in East Pakistan and
were met by various Liptonians and escorted back to our home, a
ground-floor flat, one of four blocks in the compound, each with four
such flats. Leslie had seen the block built, and had taken great pains
with the décor and furnishings to greet his fiancée (a few years
earlier!). Actually it had been another fiancée, but on the ship coming
out to marry Leslie in Calcutta, she met another man and married him
instead. It was pretty brutal, for the wedding was only a week away, and
the poor groom had to give back all the presents, un-order the cake
and do other dreary chores, but they say it's an ill wind that blows
nobody any good, and he made do with me in the end and we were
all happy.

As a new bride and new to the country, all the wives were very kind
in welcoming me and vied with each other in giving large coffee
parties, each successive one providing more food than the last. By
Chittagonian standards, I was pretty lacking in social graces. I didn't
play tennis (cartilage trouble at school ended my brief attempts to get
anywhere near the ball), bridge was a closed book to me and I was
determined it should remain that way. Mah Jong I had heard about
vaguely, but that was all, so all I could offer to Chittagong society was
my witty self and canasta. I remember being taken one morning to a
Bridge, Mah Jong and Canasta drive at someone's home. As we drove
up the hill to the imposing mansion at the top, I innocently remarked

what a nice block of flats it looked and was gently told that it was in fact a house belonging to some very important wife in the Chittagong hierarchy. When we arrived, there were masses of chattering women, lots of them in stockings and probably corsets, and I was relegated to the lowest grade of play, Canasta. I was so thrilled that I knew how to play, and it was a bitter blow when I found they played a much harder version called Samba, and I wasn't allowed to do half the things I'd been used to, apart from a few extra rules we'd put in ourselves in the family.

I was also persuaded to join the local church wives' group, which entailed sewing small and incomprehensible garments for poor children. A year at Queen's had failed to make me a really efficient needlewoman, though I tried so hard I nearly burst, and poor Miss Wyatt was forced to say, 'Jenny, you hold your needle like a sword.' Well, it was a battle – to me, at any rate.

We knew we were to be in Chittagong for only three months, and then we were due to go to Calcutta, so we didn't really mind the short-comings of the place. We had our tape recorder and masses of music to play on it, and we went sometimes to the Club for the weekly film, which was always entertaining, because if the film was dull, at least they usually got the reels in the wrong order, and you had a hilarious time trying to sort out the plot. At weekends we used to go on the beach, which was 40 minutes' drive away. The sand was pretty muddy and the sea not exactly a tropical clear blue, but we had fun all the same. One time, I was running in shallow water and cut my foot open. Leslie leapt into the waves and gallantly carried me out. We wrapped the wound in his handkerchief and, still bleeding copiously, began to drive back to find the doctor as it was obviously going to need stitching. We had quite a ride, because Leslie had been feeling adventurous on the way there and had gone up and down several steep banks. Somehow, the Land Rover found them harder returning than coming. We stuck once, and had to be pushed out by the local population, who appear like magic when needed, but mostly when not.

Chittagong boasted two doctors, one an excitable Viennese with a hoarse voice, the other a missionary. With an entertaining lack of professional etiquette, the first medico would pour out all sorts of indiscretions about his ecclesiastical rival, and tell us about the dreadful crimes carried out on long-suffering patients. I never knew the missionary medico, but a friend of mine used to go to him and gave a spirited impression of the good man searching in a dusty cupboard for medicine, finding a bottle, peering at it, inspecting the label, and then saying he thought two teaspoonfuls a day would do, but on second thoughts, no, perhaps better take three to be on the safe side . . .

Several hours later I left the surgery, enriched with three stitches and a tetanus jab. It had taken a long time to accomplish all this because, as the good doctor explained, he couldn't have his fan on at the same time as the sterilizer, and anyhow, the power was very low then. Luckily, it wasn't actually off. We used to get a lot of blackouts, which forced the residents of the flats up on to the cool of the flat roof.

Not long after we had to call in the doctor again when Leslie got jaundice. We had just been up to the Chittagong Hill Tracts, and had spent the weekend in the dak bungalow there at Rangamutti. This was an oil-lit, thatched residence, with hard iron beds, thunderboxes (loos!), and everything cooked in coconut oil served by two children. We blamed Rangamutti for the jaundice and Leslie was sent to bed to rest for two weeks on a fat-free diet. Now at last I am coming to the point

Making soup on safari in the Chittagong Hill Tracts, 1955.

of the whole story. It was while Leslie was laid low that we received an
invitation to lunch aboard the *Magdala*, a Danish ship which was in
port. These lunch invitations were much sought after by the European
population in Chittagong, for the country had ceased all imports of
foods and luxuries some time before. We had a Danish friend, Hugo
Hansen, who worked for the East Asiatic Shipping Company and he
asked us to this lunch. Poor Leslie nobly declined but kindly said I
could go, so we left him to his boiled chicken and went off to our
smorgasbord.

We were all sitting on deck after this magnificent lunch when the
talk got round to dogs. The Captain casually mentioned that the ship's
cook had been given a dog by his girl-friend when the ship was
docked in Calcutta. However, he said, the Company didn't really allow
dogs on board, so could we be kind enough to take the animal with us
and – er, well, just get rid of it??!! My protective instinct rose in a
blinding flash, and I said quiveringly, 'Could we see this dog?'
'Certainly,' said the Captain, and sent a steward off hot-foot. 'Oh dear',
I thought, 'it's sure to be some ugly great pi-dog, but we can't just
abandon it', which was clearly the Captain's idea. The door opened at
last to admit the steward with a furry bundle in his arms, which he
deposited at my feet. As I put out a hand to stroke it, the object rolled
over and presented an off-white hairy stomach. 'Oh Lor,' I thought, 'it's
a bitch!' We offered her a sugar lump and she righted herself in order
to refuse it and sat on my lap happily. I was simply thunderstruck at the
whole business. Here was the dog of my dreams – for I have always
loved hairy mongrels – mine for the asking. 'Please, Hugo, I must have
her. Can you ask the cook if it's all right?' Good naturedly, Hugo went
off to negotiate, for the steward had an idea that the cook was already
intending another home for her. While Hugo was gone, I just sat and
gloated over my new treasure. She was quite small, about 10 inches
high at the shoulder, black, with a white ruff, legs, tail-tip and chest.
There were two irregular white patches on either side of a black shiny
nose, and a magnificent beard and eyebrows covering nice dark eyes.
The left forepaw was slightly crooked, and in later life developed a
slight limp, presumably from an early accident. We subsequently found
she had a very good voice for her size, and didn't have that irritating
yap which so many small dogs possess. She has a very happy
appearance, with her plumed tail curled over her back. We have often

*Myself with Skipper on the veranda the
day we got her. Chittagong, 1955.*

been asked what breed she is, and we are stumped for an answer. I have
recently met a Lhasa Apso who has some resemblance, so I think there
may be some of that in her, or Tibetan Terrier, with perhaps a dash of
Shih Tzu; a very exotic cocktail, and not one that can be easily
duplicated.

A leash suddenly dropped into my lap. I looked up and Hugo was
grinning down at me. 'It's all fixed. She is about six months old.' And
that is the sum total of all we know of Skipper's life before we got her
– or rather she got us! I have so often wondered about her first home.
She was obviously not bred by a professional, for she has not one, but
two dew claws on each hind leg. I have to keep them cut short or they
tangle with each other, and with a yell she stands helpless until I rush
to unhook her! Various vets have offered to remove them, but they are
so much a part of her appearance, and that rear view, with its swivel
walk on those odd paws would never be the same without them.

Shortly afterwards, we said farewell to the *Magdala*, and drove back
to tell Leslie the good news. It was lovely to have a dog again; my last
one, a Yorkshire Terrier, had had to be put to sleep in 1942 and we had

never had another. We were loaded with apples for Leslie, a real luxury, and our new passenger leant out of the Land Rover and took a great interest in the passing scene. This mostly consisted of a lot of bloody carcasses hanging up, with interested onlookers, for it was Idd, the end of Ramadan, when there is feasting and celebration and even the poorest family buys a goat and slaughters it. For the previous few days there had been a succession of doomed animals passing the flat on the road, which upset me.

We arrived home and Hugo went into the bedroom first and cunningly plied the invalid with sweet talk and apples. When he was suitably mellowed, I carried in my new friend.

'That's rather nice,' (typical male understatement, but for him, pretty effusive).

'Yes, actually, she's ours . . .'

He only put up a token resistance: the usual 'What-about-when-we-go-on-leave, is-it-house-trained? Why-a-bitch?' obbligato, but he knew he was beaten. He contented himself, between mouthfuls of apple snow, with issuing Sensible Male Dictums. She must sleep in the bathroom, none of this sleeping with us lark. I didn't argue, but felt that Skipper was capable of fighting her own battles. When bedtime came, I dutifully shut her in the bathroom with a box of straw. I just had time to climb into bed before she began to whine and scratch the new paint . . .

'Perhaps if I tie her up, but leave the door open,' I suggested brightly to the hummock in the next bed.

Back between the sheets, I listened to her reproachful whining. Then I crept in to her, put her in the box, put the box by my bed, and we all went to sleep.

Next morning she made a vast puddle in the spare room in spite of repeated walks. I suppose it was the nearest to a deck that she could find, but after that one lapse, she lost her sea-legs and took to doing it on grass like any other dog. There was one place, however, that she could never be persuaded to pass. This was a bungalow nearby occupied by a passionate French couple. We used to watch them wrapped in torrid embraces on the veranda; they were always doing it. Anyhow, we could never get Skip to pass the place. She would put her tail down and scuttle back homeward. She looked equally miserable when, in wet weather, I tried to make her wear a plastic mackintosh.

She sat and whined, then scuttled a few yards on three legs, using a fourth to scratch frantically at the offending garment under her tummy. She hated it so much, I gave up, and she never wore a coat again until we went to Nairobi, where it was quite cold sometimes.

After the usual chaos of tea-chests, wood wool and newspaper, we packed up and left Chittagong for Calcutta on August 11th, 1956. Skip travelled serenely on my lap all the way in an ancient Dakota; I doubt if Pakistan International Airways is quite so easy-going these days! The only formality connected with her departure was her Health Certificate. This we had obtained from a vet in town. He had viewed her with deep suspicion from behind his desk, at a safe distance. In the rather dim light, and at that range, I doubt if he could have seen much, but he duly wrote that the dog of Mrs Pierson was free from infectious diseases etc., and received fifteen rupees for his trouble. After all that, nobody ever once asked to see it and we might just as well have saved our money. (In those days a rupee in East Pakistan was worth two shillings and tuppence – about 12p nowadays.) We left the office with our Pathan best man, Alan Sher, in charge.

For the first week in Calcutta we lived in the Grand Hotel, for the Auckland Square flat was not quite ready for us. We had a vast room overlooking Chowringhee, Calcutta's main street, full of trams, bullock carts, hooting buses and sweating coolies pushing hand-carts. During the day, of course, Leslie would depart to the office to perform his rituals over the tea-pots; it was some months before I actually discovered exactly what he did there. A tea-taster seems to have a strange fascination for some people.

'But how interesting,' they say, 'I suppose he can't smoke or drink.'

I'm forced to admit this is a fallacy, and I have yet to meet a tea-man who is a teetotaller and very few are non-smokers. In fact the ritual of tasting still fascinates me, and I still have to stifle an irreverent tendency to giggle. First the tea is brewed in special pots, with a measured amount of tea and milk, but no sugar. After allowing it to stand for six minutes, the taster approaches, a minion behind him wheeling a tall brass spittoon. With due ceremony, a spoon is produced from the breast pocket of the white coat all tasters wear. This spoon looks to the layman like a soup spoon, but no, it is a tasting spoon. A mouthful of tea is scooped up and 'thrown back on to the palate', as it is grandly described. They don't add that this entails the sort of sucking and

clooping noises that in the old days would have sent you from the
nursery with a king-size flea in the ear from Nanny. This rather
revolting rite accomplished, the mouthful is spat in an accurate jet into
the spittoon and some wise comment is passed to an acolyte, who then
writes it down for posterity. The High Priest then moves majestically
on to the next pot, sometimes pausing to sniff at some of the
unbrewed loose tea which lies on a piece of paper by each pot. This
sometimes leaves the High Priest with tea leaves on his nose, but still
no one laughs and the procession shuffles on until the end of the line
is reached. Perhaps now you can understand the fascination I still feel
for the tea trade. Time cannot dim the joy I get in hearing that one lot
is 'Bright, useful' or 'Thick and Coloury' or perhaps 'Over valued' (that
is, the broker's idea of what it's worth doesn't coincide with the taster's
valuation). The most pathetic dismissal for a tea is merely to have 'o/c'
written beside its catalogue number. This means 'out of condition' and
that it tastes awful to an expert, though you and I might not notice the
difference. Personally, I seldom drink tea and most of them taste the
same, but it's nice to know some people can even tell where a tea has
been grown, and one hopes the ritual atmosphere that surrounds a
tasting session will never be replaced by computers or robots.

Skip in Calcutta, November, 1955.
She always had the crooked paw.

In Auckland Square, Calcutta, 1955.

While Leslie was bowed over his tea-pots, Skipper and I used to take a taxi to the flat we were going to live in. It was a decayed-looking building, of the hue best described as Calcutta red, a sort of terracotta orangey brick paint, used to embellish most of the bigger houses in Calcutta. It had lovely marble floors but I sometimes wonder if the weight of them hasn't pulled the old place down; it was pretty rickety even twelve years ago. It had a marvellous view across the tank, an artificial lake surrounded by flame trees, which in the season, would be almost bowed with the weight of the huge scarlet blooms. After we moved in, we found there was always some drama going on in the square. One morning we heard shouts and yells and running feet and saw a wild-eyed man pelting past with a knife in his hand. There was a gaggle of chaps after him, throwing bricks and stones and yelling blue murder. Another time an old lady who was washing in the tank was robbed of her necklace, and the excitement was tremendous, though no one was caught. I once watched some poor chap who must have been stealing something being beaten up by the gardeners in the square. They tore his shirt off and kicked him and he fled as soon as he could get up.

The tank was also a meeting place and club for many of the local population. Gossip was exchanged, washing was done, being slapped into cleanliness on a big stone, fish were caught, heads were de-loused and the local bad girl used to make pickups there. In the wet season, the level would rise alarmingly and Skip and I could hardly get round for our walk. Our porch outside the flat used to flood too, and I shall never forget poor Skipper's face when I brought her down one morning and indicated that what had to be done must be accomplished in six inches of muddy water. She waded in obligingly, but it obviously wasn't her idea of fun!

Her main recreation in the square was to stalk crows. The Indian House Crow is a big, noisy, bullying bird, and his harsh cawing is a constant background noise in Indian life. Skip was convinced she could catch one and used to select her victim as it bounced about the grass. Then she would creep up very slowly and carefully, but apparently convinced she was invisible to her victim. The latter would pretend not to see her, but would send a telepathic message to a nearby pal or two, who would creep up behind the hunter from the rear. The climax would come without fail when the rear attacker, with a bounce and a tweak, pinched her tail and flew off with a triumphant caw. Poor Skip – she always looked so bewildered each time, and never learnt to guard her rear! Sometimes five or six would gather round, just out of range, and jeer at her, and on one occasion I was mobbed by dozens because I was holding a single flight feather from a kite that I had picked up. They have a special alarm call when one is killed or injured, and every crow within earshot comes to join in. On this occasion a great flock followed me round the square shouting abuse until I got home. Most odd, when you consider it wasn't even their species. I tried holding up the feather and the cawing doubled in volume, they were so upset. I was so fascinated by this that I went out again some days later with a different feather, and again they all rallied round to tell the world how wicked I was.

One hot day, just before we moved into the Auckland Square flat, Skipper and I were returning to the hotel at lunch time. We couldn't find any taxis in the usual places, so we had to walk all the way. It was very hot and poor Skipper soon began to wilt; down went her tail, a sure sign she is scared or tired, and I suddenly realised that the pavements must be scorching her paws. I carried her the rest of the way and when we reached Chowringhee, I realised why there were no taxis. It was a hartal day. This means a sort of general strike for one day.

Shops close or risk being broken up, buses won't run, and the hooligan element has a heyday. I even found the hotel bolted and barred, and finally got in through the side entrance. Leslie was already back and we went up to the balcony of our room to watch what went on. A lot of people were roaming about shouting slogans, one chap was knocked off his bike and a car or two was bounced, but compared with past hartals, it was pretty quiet.

Not long after our arrival in Calcutta, I attended my first company cocktail party, in honour of a visiting director out from London. At the time I thought, 'Who was Mr Lipton, anyway?' a pretty good sort of question to keep the conversation rolling, and I was surprised at the hurt amazement that greeted my innocent query. A kind friend offered to lend me Alec Waugh's book about Sir Thomas Lipton, our founder, and I then realised that it wasn't really a very sensible question to ask. However, I wasn't the only member of the Pierson clan to put up a black at that party. Leslie distinguished himself, though less publicly than I, by being sick in the Tea Department Manager's flower-bed after one whisky. This was poetic justice, because he was still supposed to be on the waggon after jaundice, and the six-months ban wasn't nearly up. All in all, quite an eventful evening.

In spite of this inauspicious start, we soon settled down to life in Calcutta. We still look back on those days with a certain amount of nostalgia, for though it is a filthy, smelly, teeming city, in many ways we liked it, especially in the cold weather, with the smoke from all the fires making the air misty. The dhobis used to dry all the washing over these fires when it was wet, and everything would come back smelling strongly of charcoal and smoke, a very special concoction I have never met since, and rather nice once you got used to it on everything.

So much has been written in recent years about India and her problems that I don't intend to go into it all here. Sufficient to say that when we were there, the problems of over-population seemed to be insurmountable. To me this is the root of all the frightful poverty of the country – that and greed in high places. It is a terrible indictment of a country that you have to force yourself to become accustomed to seeing hundreds of people who have no homes, and whose bed each night is the pavement. There they lie, men, women and children, wrapped as best they can in rags in the cold weather, sweating it out if it is hot, and as you come out of the cinema, you step over them.

Beggars are so numerous, it is impossible in many cases to give to them or you are surrounded in no time. The huge-eyed children, with pot bellies, run beside you with their eternal cry, 'No mamma, no pappa, gimme four annas'. With the people in this state, what hope for the animals? Skeleton bullocks staggering along with their tongues literally hanging out, tottering ponies pulling old-fashioned carriages with brass lamps on them, their harness held together with string and wire and they themselves covered in sores; sad-eyed, furtive pi-dogs with no hair; panting chickens carried head down in big bunches – there was no end to the agony of it. There was a part of the market where one could buy almost any creature: rabbits, rats guinea pigs, parakeets, mynahs, deer, pigeons – I even saw a small tiger cub once. They were all overcrowded, badly fed and unhappy, despite the efforts of an overworked and understaffed S.P.C.A. I used to help in a clinic where poor people could get free treatment for their sick animals, the only one of its kind in Calcutta. When I left, the idea had caught on and it was well attended.

I still get a kick out of recalling the time when I stopped a man from goading a very small calf that was too young to walk far. The mother cow and her owner were ambling along Chowringhee – on the pavement of course – and luckily going the same way as I was. I watched grimly as the calf tottered along, helped by a hefty wallop or a twist of the tail, and finally forced myself to interfere. The man must have understood even my limited Hindi, for he picked up the calf and proceeded to carry it. As he was going my way, with great glee I followed the little procession for quite a way, and when I finally left them, I noticed with unholy joy that the calf had made a large wet patch all down the man's shirt. The sad thing about all this is that so much of the cruelty is not deliberate, it is just sheer thoughtlessness. It simply does not occur to a starving Indian with a living to earn that an animal can feel too. I fear it will be a very long time before animals get a square deal from Man, even those who are his very livelihood.

CHAPTER 3

1956 – Four months in Cochin and visits to Ooty

THE PIERSONS SAW IN THE New Year of 1956 with a new sort of party. We had had enough of the usual all-stand-round-and-scream-at-each-other-through-the-smoke sort of party, and we determined to do something different. We therefore devised a 'travenger hunt'. This was a cross between a treasure hunt and a scavenger hunt and was as good a way of risking death or disablement as has ever been invented. It was ambitiously planned for five teams of three each for the fifteen guests. Each team had separate treasure clues, all in the flat, but the scavenging clues were common to both teams. These two sorts of clues alternated, so that one moment a participant might be tearing out to the square to find some duckweed, the next moment he would be searching the bookcases for Churchill's *The Gathering Storm*. Leslie and I, as hosts, had the best job, that of refereeing the various objects brought for our inspection. (Could that moribund fly REALLY be called Something Live in a Matchbox? and did this bus ticket number really end in a four underneath all the mud on it?) To ensure a rousing start to the evening, we made the first clues send all five teams to the bathroom. Each team had a box with five matches inside it, and that was their only means of illumination for the bath room and adjoining bedroom. It was quite entertaining to watch our guests milling around in the semi-darkness, searching under the bath, in the cistern, under the seat and in the medicine cupboard. I rather think we were a bit unpopular with our neighbours; I know one household had their dinner interrupted by a dishevelled couple in their kitchen demanding last Tuesday's *Statesman*. The potted plants on the staircase were ransacked for earthworms and water dripped liberally on the landing from duckweed we had requested from the tank. Each team also had one anagram to decipher, but here I was too subtle for one team. Biddy Perkins came panting up to tell me she had searched EVERYWHERE for an ALEEPOSING PALM, and there wasn't one to be found in the whole of Calcutta! She was more than a little chagrined when I told her to try the Anglepoise Lamp for the next clue! We rounded off a strenuous evening with soup and baked potatoes with cheese, and everyone seemed to have had a good time. In fact we did it again the year after.

Just as we were settled in, we were told that we would be posted to Cochin for four months to take over from Stan Holland, an old friend of Leslie's. Stan was going on three months' leave to the U.K. and was also getting married. I had a hazy idea that Cochin was (a) in China or (b) a breed of fowl with feathered trousers. I was wrong about the first and right about the second: there is a trousered fowl called a Cochin-China, hence the confusion in my mind. Cochin is, in fact, a pleasant port in South India.

The evening of February the 8th found us all packed up and facing the noise and bustle of Howrah Station. We had berths booked on the Madras sleeper, which it would take us two days and a night to reach. Then we had to change at Madras for the train to Cochin. The journey was to take from Wednesday evening to Saturday midday, so you can imagine my concern for Skipper. Officially, no dogs were allowed in the compartments – they had to travel in the guard's van – but I was determined to spare Skipper that doubtful pleasure. Leslie managed to get one of the office clerks to nobble the guard and for Rs.20(about thirty shillings) we were told Skipper could travel with us. In a country as poor as India, you can get most things by greasing the relevant palm!

As we piled into the carriage, I was somewhat daunted to see a large 'No dogs allowed' notice and I ducked guiltily into our compartment, Skip clasped to my bosom like an illegitimate baby. Luckily, she was very good; she curled up in a corner and slept. We shouted our farewells to Hugo as we chuffed noisily on our way, and settled down to enjoy the trip.

After about five hours had passed, I began to worry about Skip getting out for a run, so I went down the corridor to see the guard. We seemed to be slowing down, so I hoped I might get our illegal passenger out for a moment. In my fluent Hindi, I enquired 'Thi kai for kutta?' with a furtive glance round to see we were not overheard. He started like a nervous racehorse, and indicated it was far from All Right for the Dog, apparently, this was far too important a stop for a small dog to emerge unobserved. Only the smallest of country sidings would suffice for this necessary descent; we must wait. And wait we did for another hour or two . . . At last we came to a small country halt and there, in pitch darkness, Skipper and I climbed down on to the line; this time she wasted no time in looking for The Right Spot, as she is sometimes maddeningly prone to do. We were safe aboard again very rapidly, for I was afraid the train might suddenly depart, leaving two lonely figures standing thunderstruck on the track.

We spent a fairly comfortable night in ingenious bunks; the top one appeared from the wall when the attendant pressed a button, and we had clean sheets and air-conditioning, most luxurious, as we found later. The following day passed uneventfully. Skip and I made our death-defying descent several times, with great success, and we spent the rest of the time looking out of the window, chatting or dozing. Our meals were taken in the dining car, which sounds a lot more magnificent than it actually was. As there was no corridor, one had to get on it at a station, and nip back smartly to our compartment when we next stopped. We fought our way through the screaming babies, food vendors, goats, dhotied gentlemen, veiled ladies and beggars, without which no station in India is complete.

You can imagine that by the time we got to Madras next evening, we were pretty dirty and tired, though in better shape than the bearer, who was accompanying us, poor chap, Second Class. He was such a nice man and had been with Leslie in his bachelor days. He had served in the British Army and enjoyed travelling about, so had been with us in Chittagong (his home) and Calcutta, and when asked, said he would like to come to Cochin too. His name was Murad Mia, but for some reason he was just called 'Bearer'. He really looked tousled as he emerged from his teeming Second Class compartment. He was very cheerful, however, and greeted Skipper especially. He had a soft spot for her, which was unusual since he was a Muslim, and in general they consider dogs unclean and often will not even touch them.

Before we climbed aboard the Cochin train, we purchased what we supposed was light refreshment for the journey in the shape of lamb sandwiches, but when we opened the packets later, we found first a layer of banana leaves, and inside a glutinous mass of cold rice sparsely dotted with small pieces of shoe-leather. We hurled this unpleasant offering out of the window and settled down with considerably less comfort than we had enjoyed on the other train. For a start there was no air-conditioning, so it got rather hot, despite the efforts of a small but frenzied fan above our heads. For this trip we had only two berths booked, not the whole compartment, so we shared it with a prolific Indian family and their sixteen (I counted) pieces of luggage. Just as we were wondering what sort of a night we would have, they all got out and only one man remained. He very soon let down a top bunk, which hung suspended by two chains against the wall, and retired early to bed. There were no sheets or blankets. I fed Skip the remains of her supply from a plastic bag, and we passed a bumpy night. I often woke up if we stopped at a station and watched all the hurley-burley outside in the moonlight. By midday Saturday we finally steamed into Cochin and we climbed thankfully down to greet Stan. He took us to the Malabar Hotel, where we were to stay until he left in a week's time. We fell thankfully into bed that night; it was marvellous not to be jolting and swaying all the time.

While Leslie accustomed himself to a new office routine, Skip and I either pottered about the hotel, where she fell accidentally into the swimming pool, or went across by launch to see our house. This was quite small, white-painted, with an orange-tiled roof, just across the road from the sea. It had a small walled garden with its own tiled children's swimming pool, which afforded us a lot of pleasure later.

I remember spending a very long time ministering to a spaniel with

1956. The house in Cochin, then the only one owned by Lipton's.

septic ears. He belonged to a friend of Stan's, a bachelor who was sharing the bungalow. He also had a black Labrador called Blarney, and both Blarney and Bonzo, the spaniel, were what I call typical bachelor's dogs, badly trained and not very well cared for. The edges of Bonzo's ears were septic, under a mass of tangles and clots of hair, and it was a nasty job to sort out. His owner asked us if we would look after him for a time as he was moving into the Club up the road until he found another chummery (this expressive word means a gaggle of bachelors living together). Blarney, whom he always favoured, was to go with him. As we had also undertaken to look after Lita, Stan's boxer bitch, we had quite a crowd of canines. Skip was overwhelmed when she was introduced, but soon got used to them. We had a lot of fun with the three of them. It was a bit like having children. They used to play 'Let's Scrag Skipper' all about the house, rugs flying, claws skittering on the tiled floors, until the quarry had had enough and went to ground unfairly under a low chair. Poor Lita, her stumpy tail all agog, would crouch, bottom in the air trying to scoop out her prey, whimpering frantically while Bonzo stood and watched approvingly. I used to take them on the beach every morning after Leslie had gone to the office. I'd listen to make sure no cars were passing, then open the big gate and let loose the pack! Over the road they streamed, Lita first, bounding athletically along, then Bonzo, screaming with excitement, ears flapping, and last of all poor Skipper pounding gamely in the rear, determined not to be left out of the fun. Once on the sand, Lita would dig for crabs, sand flying in all directions until she caught the unfortunate beast and tore it to bits. On one occasion, however, the tables were turned on her. For some reason, she decided not to kill her prey in the usual way, and instead she flopped over and rolled on it! The crab, who was no fool, clamped on to her shoulder and she leapt up and spun round in circles, generally looking very stupid while I sat on a rock and laughed till I cried. She was also a keen swimmer, hurling herself into the waves and paddling out to sea. On one occasion I got really worried. She was chasing a gull and she went so far out after it, I was up to my hips in the water calling frantically. It seemed like a lifetime before she finally gave up the futile chase and turned round.

Skipper loved the beach but was no good at blood sports. You only had to point at a perfectly virgin patch of sand and say 'Look, seek it!'

for her to start digging like mad, only surfacing at intervals to get her breath, sand all over her nose and tongue. It was on the beach there that she had her first asthma attack, although at the time I didn't realise what it was. She stood with her head bowed, fighting for breath, snorting and gasping, her ribs heaving, nostrils distended. It was most worrying, but after five minutes she would be off, perfectly all right. Later a vet told me there was very little that could be done to help. Luckily she has such attacks only rarely. The beach often causes it because she gets so excited, apart from all the sand she must inhale.

After the morning walk I used to rinse the dogs in the swimming pool. Lita loved it and leapt in and out with great enthusiasm, but poor Bonzo wasn't too keen, and couldn't get out without help. I have a snap taken of him peering mournfully over the edge, clinging by his front paws waiting for some kind soul to rescue him. Skipper hated the rinse too and had to be forcibly launched, and would then paddle about frantically looking for a foothold until I helped her out. At the weekends Jusey, the gardener, used to clean the pool out and Leslie and I used it. We invented our own kind of water polo, using a tennis ball, which, after a heavy beer and curry lunch session on a Sunday, tended to make the game rather hectic.

We were very lucky to do two trips up-country to Ootacamund, affectionately know to all as Ooty. Being over 7,000 feet up in the Nilgiri Hills, Ooty was much treasured in the old days as a refuge from the heat of the cities. It has a long history from the Colonial days, and the Ooty Club has ancient photos of the Hunt (jackals, not foxes) and a venerable atmosphere. We stayed at the Savoy Hotel, in our own little Iris Cottage with huge geraniums growing by the door. The nearby Wenlock Downs made us marvel, they were so like home, with trout streams, gorse bushes, and white sheep (local ones were usually brown). There were also mimosa trees, and we spent our first wedding anniversary picnicking by the trout stream under the mimosa while I read aloud from David Niven's book, *Round the Rugged Rocks*, having terrible giggling fits at his description of how not to get a cup of coffee from an automatic machine.

We used to have morning coffee at the coffee shop and admire the Botanical Gardens with its bandstand. Then back to the hotel to a panelled dining room full of hunting prints and with a roaring fire in

Wenlock Downs, Ooty, 1956.

the bedroom. It all made a wonderful, peaceful break from the heat of Cochin.

Life in Cochin was pretty quiet most of the time, but one day I was sitting on the veranda reading when there was the most colossal bang and the whole house seemed to get up and shake itself. Every dog in the district began to bark dementedly, Lita and Skipper were petrified, and only Bonzo seemed unmoved. I had vaguely noticed a red flag flying by the beach, but no one had told me it meant the navy was having gunnery practice. Poor Lita – she was a pitiful sight, and she never got used to it. Panting, goggle-eyed and shivering, she used to run off and hide, usually in the most unsuitable places where there was no room, such as under the store cupboard. The bearer was very concerned about her, and on one occasion I found her palpitating under a bed with a yellow duster tied round her ears, looking like an unusually paralytic mumps case. If the red flag went up before Leslie went to the office, he used to take Lita with him so as to get a bit further away from the din.

After a time Lita came in season and we told David he would have to remove Bonzo, so reluctantly he moved to the Club to join Blarney. However, he kept on coming back to us. I think David used to take the more favoured Blarney to the office with him so naturally Bonzo came back to the house. He would arrive at all hours, digging holes under the gate, howling and generally being an awful nuisance. We asked David to keep him shut up, but nothing seemed to be done to control him and when he finally woke us at 5.30a.m. with his mournful howls, we decided to do something drastic. We got dressed, collected the unhappy suitor, and led him back to the Club. We crept into David's room, which was on the ground-floor, through the French windows, which he had left wide open with just a chair across them. I imagine this was supposed to keep Bonzo in – a vain hope indeed. Leslie picked up Bonzo, and carried him in to the bedroom, where he then dumped him on to his sleeping master. Poor Bonzo scrambled about on the bed, putting his great paws into David's face before he finally leapt off. David sat up in a great umbrage but we just said, 'Here's your dog, now perhaps you'll keep him under control,' and marched out, feeling victorious! We had also noticed with glee the liberal amount of muddy paw-marks which now decorated some-body's sheets and pillow-case . . . Strangely enough, after that Bonzo never returned to the bungalow, which just goes to show that it pays sometimes to be nasty!

Poor silly old Bonzo! He was a victim of what I call bachelor non-dog-lovers. I have met many of them out East. They profess to love dogs but keep them at home when they are at the office all day, left to the servants to feed and care for. Just up the road from us there was just such a dog, a daschund. I think he was one of those poor dogs that 'goes with the house'. Anyway, I found him one morning on the beach, his eyes picked out by the crows, very dead indeed. I was so angry and upset I wrote a furious letter to his so-called owner, describing the corpse and blaming his carelessness, for the gate was always left open and the dog used to wander at will. I got an angry chit back telling me to mind my own business, but I felt slightly better after expressing myself on paper.

One pouring wet day, after Leslie had come home from the office, Lita, still in season, got out and went off husband hunting. We dashed off in the car to hunt for her and finally found her gambolling in the rain with Blarney. we never dreamt that the worst could have happened in such a short time and in all that rain, but I'm afraid that nine weeks later the Hollands reaped the doubtful benefits of our carelessness in the shape of several black pups.

Lipton office bids us farewell on leaving Cochin in 1956. Sitting: Mr E.L. Durham, Mrs S.Y. Holland, Mr and Mrs L.G. Pierson, S.Y. Holland Esq. (Manager), Miss V.A. De Cruz. Standing: First Row: Messrs. V.P. Bhat, M.D. Aloysius, G.V. Pai, R. Zacharian, T.S. Raghavan, V.G. Amon. Standing Second Row: Messrs. G.I. Antony, T.L. William, T.S. Kamalakaran, M.B. Kassim, and Lita, the Hollands' Boxer.

Our stay in Cochin was ending. We had enjoyed our four months, though we found the social life pretty exacting. I am not a drinker and can get through an evening quite happily on one whisky and soda. This was quite inexplicable to many of the Cochin socialites and I got very tired of being constantly pressed to have 'One for the road' (surely that phrase vies with 'Long time no see' as the emptiest of all social inanities!). I also got sick of the wolves. The first party we went to, I was tentatively mauled by the Pack Leader, but the general attitude was 'Don't mind old —, he's always like that, ha, ha.' Well, to my way of thinking, there are some who can maul and some who can't. I prefer not to be clasped in a stifling grip while dancing, but the gentleman in question was very tight and very sure he was the original answer to the Maiden's Prayer. However, this was very small beer compared to another party we went to later during our tour. We had Gone On, a common event after a party. Someone says 'Come on, were Going On to so-and-so's' so you gather your weary body, wish you had worn sensible shoes, and hope your voice won't give out completely after two hours' shouting through a thick fog of tobacco smoke. On this occasion we Went On to a singularly unattractive bachelor's house. Our host was greasy, drunk and just not my type. My dress was too tight, it was eleven, and I had foolishly ordered dinner at the house, so it was the last straw when mine host seated himself opposite me on a small table and then proceeded to stroke my thighs. I kept fending him off and sending meaningful glares at Leslie, but it seemed a lifetime before we escaped and went home to an unwanted and over-cooked supper. Funnily enough, the last time I had been pawed in public was on a London Bus between Baker Street and Park Lane. I have never been so astonished in all my life. The sheer nerve of it took your breath away. There I was, on a fine spring day, sitting on the seat by the exit clutching an envelope of X-rays to deliver to a doctor, when a funny feeling came over me. I stole a glance at my neighbour, a thin, sickly young man with a mackintosh over his lap. His right hand, nearest me, was hidden in its folds, and then I saw that my skirt seemed rather rucked up. I sat there, paralysed with disbelief, as a hand got as far as my suspender. After all, what does one do? Shout out, 'Look, this man is stroking my thigh'? Clasp the hand in question and show the rest of the bus it really is there? Turn to him and make an icy comment? Slap his face? As you might guess, all I did was get out at my stop and give him an awful glare before removing my jellied knees to the safety of the street. Some days later I saw him again, sitting next to a girl near the front, mac in place, and she got out pretty rapidly at the next stop! They say it takes all types to make a world, but you can see why I like animals, can't you?

CHAPTER 4

Cochin ducks, U.K. leave
and Calcutta pregnancy

STAN HOLLAND WAS DUE BACK with his new wife Margaret in mid-June, and then we were to fly to the U.K. for three months' leave before returning to Calcutta. For some reason I suddenly decided to buy a duck to decorate the swimming pool. I went out to the market and for just over four shillings, I chose a rather grubby off-white duck with a yellow bill. She improved immensely with good food and lots of baths, and we called her Augusta. The dogs were fascinated but if they got too close, they got a sharp jab from her bill, so they used to watch from a safe distance as she bathed and splashed in the pool. Just before the Hollands arrived, I went out and bought a mate for her, a handsome drake with the usual curly tail and green shiny head. We kept them in the garage at night and each morning we used to watch the dash to the pool when they were let out. George unfailingly asserted his marital rights as soon as they entered the water, the whole process being rounded off by baths all round! Some time later we got a letter from the cook, Raman, which I here quote in full, because I think it is a gem, and it has pride of place in my scrap book.

Respected Master and Madam,

I happened to know through my present Master and Madam that Master and Madam has arrived at Calcutta and have immense grief in the inability of sending a letter to know your whereabouts. It was only due to my constant work and present circumstances. So, first of all I beg to pardon me.

Now for the sake of Almighty I and my co-workers are working here without any annoyances and Master and Madam are very obliging to us. Madam's two ducks are carrying on their daily routines without any resistances and enjoying a pleasure life.

All servants from bungalow have conveyed their best regards to Master and Madam. I am getting well and have immense desire to come and see Master and Madam if God will assist and circumstances will prevail. Daily I pray to God to make an occasion like that and to give Master and Madam prosperity for a long time.

Saying my humble wishes to Master and Madam, I terminate this letter.

Your most obedient servant

Raman (cook)

I think that is the nicest letter we have ever had. For sheer simplicity and unspoilt genius, it stands alone. What could better describe the life the ducks led? We knew their daily routines, and the pleasure life! We had a very soft spot for Raman and on the last day before we left Cochin, he told me he wanted to give us a special lunch which he would pay for. We had a marvellous meal of cold ham (which was then fifteen shillings a pound) and Christmas pudding complete with brandy butter, which sat a little heavily during our flight, but we were most touched by the whole idea. We were also given garlands of frangipani by the other servants. What a wonderful lot they were, always eager to please, none of this attitude of 'It's-not-my-job-to-do-that'. When our bearer slipped and hurt his ankle, the garden boy laid the table, the cook took him off to hospital in a rickshaw, the driver asked if we would like him to wait at table. It was wonderful how they rallied round.

Two days before we left, Skipper and the bearer set off on the long journey back to Calcutta. Other Lipton friends of ours there, Sheila and David Marsh, were going to keep Skip for us until our return in September. This time poor Skipper would have to go in the guard's van, so I tried to make her as comfortable as possible. I made her a cushion, filled a plastic bag with chopped meat, gave her a bath, and she was all set. I was horrified to see her cage. It was big enough for a Great Dane, with thick bars and a vast ring screwed to the wall, to which the guard indicated we should tie her. I refused this, because I felt she might get tangled with the lead and hurt herself. There was a small door that opened from the cage to the platform. It had no lock, and I had nightmare visions of it coming undone and her falling out. I felt an awful traitor as I put her inside on her cushion, and the puzzled face peering through the fringe and bars was most harrowing. Later I heard from Sheila that when she arrived, Sheila didn't recognise her. She was on the lookout for her and she saw a man in the compound with a bedraggled black dog. It was the bearer she recognised, not Skipper! However, after a bath and a meal she was her old self again

Skip staying with David and Sheila Marsh while we were on leave.

and did her best to keep the Marshes amused until our return. They were intrigued and a little worried about one of her odd habits. Often before she lies down, instead of the usual circling some dogs do, Skip digs. She puts her nose very close to the ground and scratches frantically with her front paws. The mystified Marshes cut her claws but still she did it, and still does. We think maybe there are malignant gremlins with pins who haunt her and have to be removed. They are very tiny, so she has to look very closely at them. Actually, the gremlins have also come to Nairobi with us, but that comes later in the story!

Back home, we spent our leave mostly in London, staying with my brother Chris or in my cousin's flat. We took a caravan round Scotland and did 1,200 miles in two weeks. It seems incredible to think we were so footloose and fancy-free, for on our next leave, three years later, we had two children!

We arrived back in Calcutta in September, and soon picked up the threads again. In November I paid a visit to the doctor, who confirmed the news that we could expect a baby in June. Someone was always pregnant in Lipton's, and I had just spent a lot of time visiting Glenys Willey, who was confined to bed in the Elgin Nursing Home expecting twins. Every day I used to go in wondering if anything had happened, but she went full term, much to her doctor's delight. Not only that, but she went so far over her time, they were in despair of her ever producing. Every day brought a new 'sure-fire' pill or injection, but at last the twins gave in and, much to everyone's relief, revealed themselves to be a boy and a girl. About this time, of course, I suspected I might be pregnant, so Glenys used to enquire eagerly each day about my condition. For years there was always a pregnant Lipton wife somewhere in Calcutta. I took on after Glenys, and Sheila Marsh took up the torch after me!

Some months later, Sheila and I were sitting on our veranda having a quiet cup of coffee when a lady was shown in by the bearer. She seemed rather agitated and was holding in one hand a birds' nesting box and in the other a small basket. She told us that she had been sent here by the vet at the animal clinic where I helped. She opened the box and inside were five very young and hideously ugly baby budgies. She told us that the mother had escaped from the aviary and that she was trying to find someone to foster them.

'You see, I'm already hand-rearing two other babies that got deserted,' and she opened the basket to show us two slightly older birds, full of life, chittering vigorously. She showed us how she fed them, using a teaspoon to shovel the seed down them, and I was surprised they had thrived on seed with the husks on. Normally baby budgies are fed on the regurgitated seeds the parents eat, which of course are husked. Naturally I couldn't refuse to help, and Sheila nobly rose to the appeal, she taking two while I took one orphan. One of hers died after a day or two, but the other grew and thrived, but one day the sweeper was cleaning the cage when the little bird took off and, to the stupefaction of Sheila, flew away over the roof tops of Chowringhee and was never seen again. Mine also thrived and we called him Tweeter. This was the hottest time of the year, April and May, and I used to go down to the Swimming Club and sit in the air-conditioned lounge. Tweeter would come with me in a small box but would be left in the Ladies Changing Rooms in case he caught a chill in the lounge. I would emerge at intervals and feed him. I wasn't entirely happy about feeding him whole seed, so I used to grind it up, using a bottle of nail polish in a tin lid, and blow off the husks. It was a long job, but the resulting yellowy dust was mixed with milk and fed to him between my finger and thumb. I tried a match-stick, and tweezers, but they were too clumsy, and we soon got the knack. A large and fascinated crowd would collect to watch us and within ten minutes Tweeter's crop would be bulging again and he would return to his cubicle of giggling ayahs, and me to the blissful cool of the lounge. He was very vocal, and in the early morning, would start to cheep frantically if I turned over too carelessly in bed. This always made the springs twang unmusically, for the bed was very old and we reckoned one of the few double-beds in Calcutta. Poor Leslie! He got fed-up at these early calls, but I explained it was all good training for the coming baby.

One hilarious day we were heading for the Club in a taxi. The driver was one of the many large and cheerful Skikhs and we were bowling along when Tweeter began to chirrup. After a few minutes we came to a halt. The driver jumped out and proceeded to lift the bonnet and search for this new mechanical problem! It was a wonderful moment when I put two and two together and showed him the culprit in his little box. The joke was much appreciated by both parties!

Tweeter eventually turned into quite a handsome bird; he was light green with yellow stripes. Skipper was very interested and we have some movie films of her hovering over him as he toddled about the floor searching for food. I taught him to fly by putting him on the book-case and standing with my hand a few feet away. He was just getting to be quite an intrepid aviator when tragedy struck. I came home one day to find a stranger in Tweeter's cage. This was a small brown finch, some type of munia that the bearer had caught in the window by Tweeter, doubtless after his seed. He had popped the intruder in with Tweeter, and the two seemed perfectly happy. As it was a large cage I had the idea of buying another pair of finches from the market and putting them in too. They were tiny, bright red with white spots, and the red was genuine. Many of the munias in the market were dyed, poor mites; you could see the dye on the cages, and innocent buyers found their birds reverting to dull brown after a few weeks. However, my birds must have brought in some disease, for one morning Tweeter was listless and weak. We were having our breakfast in the veranda where his cage hung when he tottered over to the bars nearest to me and dropped dead. I remember so vividly that I was eating a fried egg; it was the most awful meal I ever had. Our only consolation was that he had died quickly.

A few weeks before the baby was due, I was sent to bed with high blood-pressure and told to rest. The temperature was over a hundred so it wasn't much fun. Leslie never came home for lunch, so it was a long day for me. The water was liable to be turned off all day, so we used to fill up the bath early, and after lunch and a nap I would immerse my whale-like body in the tepid water and read for hours or watch the baby kicking me. Then back to bed, and gosh – it was hot! The bearer used to shut the shutters after lunch, which helped a little, and the ceiling fan was full on, whirring away, but even so, a wet patch would form on the pillow under your head. During this time we looked after Whiskey, who was a white rabbit belonging to the Perkins, our Tea Department Manager. Whiskey was a house-rabbit, and was pretty well house-trained. When the Perkins first got her, they were a little dubious as to how she would fare with Jill, their bull terrier. They needn't have worried. Whiskey gave the inquisitive Jill a smack on the nose to show her who was master and that was that! The poor doctor, on a visit, was a bit startled when Whiskey emerged from under my bed to greet him. A house rabbit is obviously a catching habit, for the Perkins are now settled in England but they still have a house-rabbit called Whiskey, who rules the kitchen with a rod of iron!

We had worked out June 25th as being The Day, and in the afternoon I was having tea with Sheila and another friend, Avril, who lived very near my doctor's consulting rooms. I happened to mention to Avril, who had a little girl of two or so, that I was getting contractions across my tummy at intervals. This caused a great stir and I was told it might be the start. Just for a lark, and as he was so near, we all sallied over to see the doctor. He gave me a quick once-over, picked up the phone, dialled and said 'Is that the Elgin? Mrs Pierson is in labour.' I can't tell you what exciting words those were! I couldn't believe it and I rushed out to tell Sheila and Avril. We took a hysterical taxi ride back to Auckland Square – the Sikh must have thought we were drunk – they left me there to pack and wait for Leslie's return from the office. I can remember vividly Avril saying to me, 'I do hope you don't mind my saying this (Good Heavens, what can she be getting at?), but I think you ought to cut your nails or you'll scratch the baby.' So I paced my flat, my lovely long talons flying about, sacrificed on the altar of Motherhood.

By six o'clock I was installed in bed, preparing for the ignominies that doctors decree shall be inflicted on the labouring mother. I had dreaded the shaving and enemas far more than the actual birth, for I was a great Dick-Read disciple and I wanted to be conscious for the birth, spurred on by Glenys, who saw both the twins arrive. I had read Dick-Read's book and done some of the exercises, and was dying to see if they would help. Several of the wives we met pooh-poohed it, and said unkindly, 'You wait!' But some of us felt that when you have waited nine months for a baby, it would be a pity not to hear its first cry and to be fully conscious, if possible. After three babies, I still feel that way. However, I never realised what hard work it would be! I have very happy memories of Neal's birth, even allowing for the fact that nature tends to make you forget the worst. Leslie had rung up about eleven, after the doctor had seen me, and was told the birth might be about seven or eight o'clock the next morning. Consequently, I don't know why he was so surprised when he was coming up the steps to see me at eight o'clock and met Dr. Preger coming out. 'I was just coming to see you,' he said, 'you've just had a son!'

I was sitting up in bed devouring a large breakfast when Leslie's face appeared round the door with an expression I can only describe as incandescent.

'I just saw him, they hadn't even had time to wash him,' he told me in awe, for he had never seen a small baby before. 'Eight pounds, six ounces – is that a lot?'

I assured him feelingly that it was a LOT. I was still recovering from some pethidine I'd been given just before the birth, which had a most unfortunate effect on me. Being by nature nosey, I had asked to see the afterbirth, and one of my vividest memories of the whole birth is looking at it and saying with a merry laugh, 'I hope that doesn't turn up at the meat market,' and subsiding into not-too-subdued giggles. I had other little verbal sallies with the poor doctor and nurses, for which I later apologised, but no one really minded. They must have been used to it, but even now it makes me cringe to think about it.

I soon settled in to the routine at the Elgin and the days passed rapidly. I had a phase of the blues after the first few days, when I was moved down a floor to the Surgical part because of a sudden rush in Maternity. I felt worst about seven o'clock in the evening after Leslie had gone and got rather weepy. Luckily, after the first day there, I discovered there was a library, and that helped to cure me. I believe I was running pretty true to type; it's the anti-climax, and the hormones sorting themselves out. However, I never had it with the other babies, I'm glad to say.

Spurred on by Glenys's positively bovine example, I was eager to feed Neal myself, and was lucky to have too much milk. They gave me stilboestril to lessen it, and I gave them pints of extra for the prem. babies. Breast-feeding is another of my hobby horses, for I find these days, fewer mothers think there is much advantage in it. At one stage, in Colombo, I was introduced to someone as 'Jenny Pierson, she has fed her baby for six months.' Apart from being far less trouble, I can't see how anyone can feel that what comes from a tin must be better than what nature provides. I realise I was lucky in being able to feed my babies with very little trouble, and I sometimes wonder if heredity helps, and if I was conditioned at all by the fact that Mummy fed us all herself (and was considered a bit of a peasant by some!). My sister Ann also fed her two, so that when my turn came, it never even occurred to me that I would not follow suit, especially with Glenys's example, as I have already quoted. I was glad not to be her. She used to tell me how, in the night, she would stand between the two vibrating cots of howling babes with the tears rolling down her cheeks, trying to make up her mind which to feed first!

After ten days they reckoned I knew enough about it all to send me home. I was most touched when we got to the flat and the bearer gave me a bunch of flowers and a furry dog, which must have cost him far more than he could afford. There was even a little card on it, which I have still got in my album: 'To baby Neil – may God bless and keep you safe through life, from Md. Murad Mia (Bearer).' My album also contains a letter from the sweeper, that was awaiting me with a bunch of flowers on my return.

'Respected Madam,

At first take my salaam both of you.

I beg to draw your kind attention with the few following lines;

That I have been working under your kind control as a sweeper for a long period with good record.

That I have received a letter from my native house that my wife is seriously ill. She has none to look after her in her bed. So I earnestly request you honour will be kind enough to grant me for 2 mths leave from 3rd July 1957.

May I therefore hope and pray that your honour will kind enough to grant me the leave for the 2 months and oblige.

Thanking you,

Yours most obediently,

Pankaj Nayak.

P. S. I am bring some flower to your honour and handover the petition to the Bearer & I left the job.'

I was sorry he had gone as he was such a good worker, with great big sad eyes and a droopy moustache. He was devoted to Skipper and would take her out for a walk twice a day, groom her, and see she was free of ticks. His replacement was a gloomy looking individual, who once enlivened our lives by sending a small piece of grubby paper to us on which was written the following magnificent message:

'I cannot come on duty today because I am to join a dinner party. Jamadar.'

Looking at the other letters as I copied the above, I found also a letter from the cook, Hussein, asking for a rise because he was a 'family man, and have 8 heads to support' and another one, written two months later, asking for another loan for his daughter's wedding 'This amount (Rs50) to be realised at installments from my salary, (After completion of my previous loans amount).'

I should perhaps explain that in most cases, these letters are written by professionals, for most of the servants were unable to write and were willing to pay a few annas to a professional scribe who would type the petition. The finest example of professional 'Blind 'em with words' was in Pakistan, when Leslie received a letter after dismissing a tea clerk as inefficient. It came from a gentleman, apparently of the legal calling, and ran as follows:

'Dear Sir,

My Client Mr —, an ex-employee of your firm, who has received by hand letter to note on 4th of June 1953, terminating his services. Instructs me to write to you as under;

1. If I annoy in the deliverance of my opinion as the chance are 'I may assume the significant fact that your FROWN over the morning talk cause this issue, as you have no other resort to dispense an advantage in your favour; wherefore you took to derive to reserve your strength to call upon against; READ 'Now lack the ability to perform the duties of a Tea Department clerk efficiently' I can quite

comprehend my client's exposition produced bitterness. Accumulation of this fact, surely would revelate itself. You have bought charge against my client with particular inference referred above and seized an opportunity to make my client appear INEFFECTIENT; wherein certainity could have no chance to prejudice. But surely according to evidence I doubt my client could be testified in your straight forward tale. You are shaking your evidence without proof. Your affirmation to; 'Now lack ability to perform duties' for such inference. My Client has been working in various branches in the Tea department without any flaw. During the space of his time. My client whom I believe to be absolutely perfect in his works. Your avocation made light of being beaten by illegal action under the semblance of 'INEFFECIENT' because these words speculate to an accurate failure in the analize of any conduct in the correct judgement of reasoning, by this mean act against my client. Wherein you have committed a wilful intent to make believe that my client is 'INEFFECIENT' thereby my client suffers loss and damage to his prosperity in life! (Now here comes the crunch, wait for it . . .)

'Whereupon my client claims damage of Rs.50,000 (fifty thousand) against you for rash and mean action in the dismissal, whilst he was winning headway in the prosperity of his daily life.

2. If the above claim for damage is not accorded forthwith I will proceed without further reference to legal action.

Yours faithfully,'

When Leslie showed me this bombshell, some months later, I asked what had he done about it?? I had awful visions of his being dragged to court, even to jail, where I could visit him as he weaved baskets . . . 'Oh, I never answered it,' he said, slightly surprised at my hysteria. 'We never heard any more, of course.' I wonder how much the poor little clerk paid, and what promises were made by the lawyer. Incidentally, in case any of you are thinking that I couldn't write a letter in Urdu if I tried for a month, you are quite right. The letters I have quoted are not just to be jeered at. In many cases they have a very apt, spontaneous twist to them, which expresses exactly what the writer means. They are quaintly picturesque, and very individual to the East, as anyone else who has lived there will tell you.

CHAPTER 5

The wedding that wasn't and problems with a new posting

I MUST ADMIT THAT MY first week of motherhood at home were quite a revelation to me. After the routine of the hospital, with Neal only brought in to me at set times, I seemed to spend most of my time at home catering for his whims and tastes! In all fairness, he wasn't really a bad baby, but there was usually a time in the evening when he just yelled, even if he was dry and fed etc. Ann had given me a copy of Doctor Spock, and I found that my son was indulging in 'irritable crying'. This helped a lot, and at least he never did it at night. I can remember the first Sunday we were home. Leslie was snoozing on the bed one afternoon whilst I struggled to please the yelling baby. Eventually, goaded by this writhing, red fiend who was trying to rule my life for me, I shook the poor creature vigorously and snarled, 'I wish you were DEAD!' Then I plonked him, screams naturally redoubled, in his cot and slammed the door. My conscience was working overtime, it was all too much, I must be an abnormal mother and I flew to Leslie and sobbed bitterly on his shoulder. After that I got better at not caring so much if he cried, and when he at last gave me a smile, I really began to get very fond of him! I have never been a 'baby-gusher' as I have always felt very young babies to be much less attractive than animals. It used to be the most embarrassing and agonising moment when a well-meaning mother said, 'I'm sure you'd like to hold him.' Even now, I don't feel a baby is really interesting until it is a few months old and can laugh and respond to you. I got a tremendous amount of pleasure in watching his growth and feeling that *I* was responsible for those firm fat thighs and big wobbly cheeks!

It was just before Neal was born that I decided to try again to find a suitable mate for Skipper, so that she too should know the joys of motherhood. I have already mentioned my first abortive attempt and my second try was not much more successful. As I didn't know any suitable dogs myself, I asked the vet at the All Lovers of Animals

Society Clinic. I used to help them with flag days, and was on the committee. It was worthwhile work, for they were the only clinic that gave free treatment to animals of the poor. The vet gave me the number of a lady who had a West Highland White Terrier, the nearest type we could find to Skipper. I rang the lady, who seemed slightly overwhelmed and informed me doubtfully that MacTavish had 'never done anything like that before' (which, knowing dogs, I doubted very much). She was also not keen on the idea of bringing Skipper to her mate, so we arranged that she would bring him round to me that afternoon. Skipper was brushed and combed ready for the nuptials, and I sweated gently, wondering what it would be like and if all would be well with my match-making. Eventually the groom arrived and was ushered in and greeted with enthusiasm by his bride. The lady and I sat down and made polite conversation, trying covertly to watch the lovers' progress without seeming to. They tore about, playfully chasing each other, then MacTavish was liberally sick on the carpet; presumably the excitement was too much for him.

'Oh dear,' said the lady, 'I gave him a drink of milk before we came out.'

I gave a bright smile, and told her not to worry and fetched a cloth and cleared up.

We waited. MacTavish continued to chase Skipper, who was getting coquettish. I was beginning to think the lady was right when she said MacTavish was a novice. Every time he looked like business, Skip would leap coyly out of the way; if she had been a girl, she would probably have wagged a finger at him and said roguishly, 'Ah, ah, now, now!'

MacTavish was sick again.

Still smiling, I cleared it up.

Both dogs then had a long drink, and refreshed, resumed their protracted courtship.

Conversation lagged. We openly watched progress, conspicuous by its absence.

MacTavish did it again, and my smile slipped a little as I trudged out to the kitchen again for the cloth.

The end came suddenly. I hardly knew what to say, but eventually, the defeated groom and his owner left us.

Skipper looked smug; not many bitches try to mount their husband instead of the more usual method, and I didn't bother to explain that maternity was not achieved that way. I was sick of the whole business and decided that such an abnormal creature deserved to remain on the shelf. It was a year or two before until I again attempted to mate her.

It was a couple of months before Neal was born that the vet told me of a very suitable mate who lived a few minutes away. He was a Lhasa Apso, and had been bred by Tenzing after his Everest triumph. I rang his owner, who was most enthusiastic, and next morning I led Skipper round to the house in Lower Circular Road. We were led into an air-conditioned study and introductions were made. Jygmeh was a most handsome dog with long golden hair, a little bigger than Skipper but the resulting pups should be marvellous, I felt. This time everything went swimmingly, though I couldn't help feeling dogs really didn't manage things very well as I sat on the floor for twenty minutes stroking a bewildered Skipper; neither party seemed very enthusiastic after the first fine careless rapture. In fact they both seemed a bit embarrassed when they finally parted. We decided to leave Skipper there for the night just to make sure. When I collected her the next day, I was told that nothing more had happened, but that Skip had pestered Jygmeh so much, he had taken refuge in his owner's bed for the night!

Certainly the movie film I took of them shows Skipper full of beans and dashing about while Jygmeh looks inscrutably oriental and dignified in a weary sort of way. Undeterred, we decided to part them for a day and bring Skipper back later. This worked like a charm. She nearly pulled my arm off going up the drive, and Jygmeh could hardly wait to be bundled into the privacy of the study.

It seems an anti-climax to record that after all our pains, there was no fluffy family gambolling about the flat a few months later! Just before we left Calcutta for Ceylon, six months later, she came in season again and we made three visits to Jygmeh, but still she had no pups. Later, in Colombo, she fell in love with Scamp, a small daschund from next door, and because it was not an arranged mating, we were sure she would have pups, but she never did. Maybe she would have made a very scatty mother anyhow.

We received the news of our posting to Ceylon in about October, 1957. We had fixed for my parents to spend Christmas with us, and as

Skip with Neal, two months old, in Calcutta, 1957.

the move was for January, we wrote and asked if they'd like to come too. Of course they were thrilled, and we were very lucky to find accommodation for them in Calcutta. The gentleman on the next floor was a grass widower, and offered us his large spare bedroom, complete with bathroom and having its own door out into the corridor. He refused to let us pay a bean.

I always enjoy getting the home ready for visitors; it makes me finally get down to doing various jobs which have been 'pending' for too long. We put up our Christmas decorations and I made my usual crib scene on the sideboard. Mummy and Poppa arrived on December 24th, a little later than planned because Poppa had to go into hospital unexpectedly for a minor operation. They were enchanted with everything they saw, loved the flat and were thrilled with their newest grandchild (by then my sister had had a boy and a girl). We had a very good Christmas lunch of guinea fowl, which was far better than turkey, and Hussein made a splendid Christmas pudding. Unfortunately, I see I have written nothing in my diary about these weeks; usually by the end of the year my enthusiasm for keeping it up has waned. Mummy has never forgotten the highlight of her Christmas, however. She was just going upstairs to bed when a party of gaily dressed drummers and dancers with jingling bells on their feet appeared in the hall. They hailed Mummy with great enthusiasm: 'Salaam, Mumee, salaam, baksheesh.' She was quite overcome but distributed the expected reward after they had performed.

Luckily the cold weather in Calcutta is from about November to February, so we needed no fans and you could even wear a sweater. It made a nice change from the hundred and ten degrees we had suffered in June! We celebrated the New Year quietly at home, wondering how we would be this time next year and how we would like Ceylon.

All too soon we were packing again. This time we were all booked to leave on a cargo boat on January 9th. It was only a five-day trip, but I was looking forward to it as my last sea voyage had been at the age of seven when we went to Denmark.

January 8th, 1958 I have marked in my diary as being an awful day! People were popping in and out all day; some were removing my three fish tanks, some were saying goodbye, one lady came to take away the aviary, only to find it wouldn't fit into her car boot. The bewildered budgies stayed outside the front door awaiting collection, Skip wandered about uneasily; Neal enjoyed the comings and goings and Leslie rang to say most of Lipton's would be coming in for a farewell drink that evening but not to worry, they would bring their own glasses! By lunch time I felt awful, aching all over, and I was gratified to find I had a temperature of 102°. I retired to bed hurriedly and my nice doctor was summoned. He confirmed I had a bad dose of 'flu and that there was no question of my travelling the next day. Despairingly I sank into the depths, moaning to Mummy, 'I suppose I shall have to stay here.'

'Nonsense,' said Mummy briskly, 'I shall stay; the men and the luggage can go on the ship and we'll follow later.' And that's how it was. That night I received my farewells from my bed rather muzzily, and from rather subdued friends, and next day glumly saw the lorry loaded with cases, the pram, boxes, Skip's bed and other impedimenta. There was a last-minute panic about Poppa's health certificate, which lacked some vital stamp and entailed a lot of dashing about for Leslie and Poppa, but they finally boarded the *Steel Traveller* and were off. That night they ran into fog on the Hoogly, and poor Skip and Leslie were kept awake by the foghorn every few minutes. Poppa, who was deaf, had taken off his hearing aid, of course, and never heard a thing. 'One advantage in being deaf,' he wrote wryly to Mummy later.

The *Steel Traveller* was American and Leslie was much amused by the informal atmosphere on board. The Captain had a dog, a daschund, and Leslie was also in charge of Gilly, the Perkins' bull terrier, for they also had been posted to Colombo Tea Department.

Our menfolk enjoyed their trip, though Leslie had a shock when he saw supper was at 5.30, because he's a late eater and likes his last meal about nine or ten o'clock! Skipper had the run of the ship and slept in Leslie's cabin and ate a lot, whilst Gilly ate less and scared the crew by her ferocious appearance (and they had never seen her crack walnuts with one crunch of her jaws!). The men went to the 'slops' and bought themselves a jaunty baseball cap each, and Leslie took a film of Poppa in his taking Skip for a walk on deck. I can't imagine what Leslie must have looked like in his, for he never wore it on dry land!

Meanwhile Mummy, Neal and I waited for Lipton's to fix us an air passage. I had spent the first two days sleeping off the flu and because of drugs, had been forced to wean Neal in one day. He was six months old so it didn't matter, but I was taking eight Stilboestril tablets a day to dry up the milk. Judging from a letter I wrote to L. on Jan. 13th, I was pretty fed up!

'God, what a bloody life this is! We are booked to leave 9a.m. on SUNDAY. I'm so fed up; I thought it would be Wednesday or Thursday after Les gave me a clean bill of health. You can't imagine how desolate it is here without all of you. I'm sick to death of alarms and excursions, comings, goings and hullos and goodbyes. I miss you horribly and hope all's well your end. Sorry to start off on such a self-pitying note, will pass on to other news! Well, I soon felt better (I could afford to be *really* ill in the time at our disposal now) & got up yesterday. The Bannocks and the Marshes came round in the morning and we nattered. Hussein (the cook) was absent all day today re a job, which he's got, and he has left straight away, which I'm a bit cross about. He was paid up to the end of the month but I couldn't stop him. Gave him a somewhat frigid farewell in consequence! The bloody downstairs cat is in season and I spend my life rushing to the window with jugs of water to dowse the yowling suitors with – great fun! (Anything is fun at the moment, I feel so bloody-minded, but it'll pass off.) Les made me wean Neal; he wallops eight ounces of milk at almost each feed, (at Rs.6 per tin!) Muk and Bubli popped in on Thur night with lovely gladioli. Bannocks sent chrysanths and Sheila came with roses AND a jar to put them in, clever of her to remember ours were all packed!

'Ma got fearfully eaten by mozzies last night and was fighting a losing battle with scarves and garments; her face was v. mottled this morning, poor dear. We have our hair done tomorrow, mine's all flat at the back from lying in bed. Mr A. has been in and out with little offerings; he says you have 'a noble face'! The bearer had to pay out Rs.12 in bribes 'cos of trouble on his visa for Pakistan, so 'spose I must repay that. What a perfectly bloody life. Being apart certainly makes you appreciate the absent half.'

However, I must have felt better after getting all that off my chest. The next letter is more cheerful; time for our departure was getting nearer and people were all very kind in looking after us.

CHAPTER 6

Now we are four!

W E LEFT AS PLANNED on Sunday and flew to Madras, where we spent one night. We all three shared a room and I remember getting very giggly with Ma because of the odd plumbing. There were masses of water pipes on the walls that made frightful noises and this, coupled with Mummy's efforts to control her mosquito net, were too much for us and we got very feeble and hysterical. She was also recovering from the sight of her first cockroach, which she had met in the bathroom . . .

Next day, we had a two-hour flight, and arrived at Colombo at midday. Poppa and Leslie brought Skip with them, so we had a real family reunion. We were thrilled at the sights of Colombo: sun, palm trees, white sands, exotic flowers, and were soon installed in the flat that Lipton's had found for us temporarily. It was on the first floor and had three bedrooms, but seemed terribly small and low-ceilinged after the Auckland Square spaciousness. Next door were the Willises of the Tea Department, and Anne was very kind in introducing me round to the other Lipton wives. One of them found me a nanny (nothing so low as ayahs here!) She was very superior, a Catholic, and had been ten years with one family and had been to England with them. She lived out but ate the same food as we did, which was expensive. Some time after my parents left, she came to me and started telling tales, in a great odour of sanctity, on the houseboy. 'I believe in taking my troubles to God, Madam, but sometimes . . .' Finally, she went sick and was told not to lift anything over ten pounds, and as Neal was about twenty pounds by then, it was an ideal way to part. She found me a new nanny, big, lazy old Joslin, whom the children loved and whom we had for the rest of our seven years in Colombo.

By April it was obvious that our family planning had slipped up somewhere, and a visit to the doctor confirmed a rather nebulous date in November. This meant altering our leave dates, but we were pleased really and hoped for a girl. The days passed quickly. I spent

'Shangri La', Colombo, 1959.

John the cook with Neal, Joslin the ayah with Sarah at 'Shangri La', 1959.

quite a lot of time at the Swimming Club or playing Mah Jong, but on May the 27th violence flared between Ceylonese and Tamil. There was fighting and a State of Emergency was declared, with a 6a.m. to 6p.m. curfew. We really knew very little about what was going on, as there was a rigid press censorship, but we heard shots and saw burnt-out huts on the Galle Road, and rumours were rife. It was not until several years later that I read Tarzi Vitachi's book, *Emergency '58*, and was horrified at the bloodshed, torture and destruction that had gone on.

One good thing about the curfew was that people living in blocks of flats got to know their neighbours, and we were very glad to have the Willises so near. We were in a cul-de-sac off Horton Place, which was a long, straight road, so that you could see if anything was coming. I used to take Skipper out for her last run at night and we would dash down the deserted road together; I used to trick Skip by turning round as soon as she shot off and running the other way; she would come to a sudden halt, realise I wasn't there and come pelting back for me, and as soon as she passed me, I would turn again. It sounds a bit feeble on paper, but out there in the moonlight, it was fun, even though I couldn't really run much with my expanding waistline. The men went to work until four o'clock each day and told us we mustn't go out of the house for there had been reports of roaming gangs of thugs only too ready to have a go at the white people.

After a few days, however, John and Biddy Perkins sallied forth with Gilly and a chap with an iron bar to protect them. They went to Colpetty market and filled their boot with all sorts of fruit and vegetables, then drove round to various Lipton houses and gave us each an assortment of produce. They refused to take any payment and we were most touched by their kindness, which I may say was very typical of them. If anyone in the company was ill, Biddy was first round with flowers and books. When I had Neal, Biddy was in the U.K., but John was round to see me in hospital with flowers and kind words of admiration for our new son. They had Skipper for us twice when we went on leave and never let us pay anything for her keep. We missed them terribly when they went to the U.K. for good in 1963, but we still see them when we go on leave, and after dear Gilly died, they bought a Lhasa Apso who looks very like Skipper indeed!

On July 11th the curfew was lifted and life went back to normal. I got German Measles for the second time in my life, but I was too far pregnant for it to harm the baby.

Then, in August, we acquired another dog.

I had hankered for a companion for Skip for some time. We both liked poodles and when an advertisement appeared in the paper for 'grey miniature poodle pup, six months, wormed and weaned,' we went tearing off to see it. We were so early, the man who was selling the pup hadn't yet arrived but his friend promised to give our address and get in touch with us. The sex of the pup was unknown, and of course we only wanted a bitch. I am a great champion of bitches and owners of dogs who suddenly find a bitch in season and go off all the time will maybe see what I mean. One friend of mine in Nairobi was astounded at the change in her Ridgeback, who for a year or so had been obedient and never wandered. Suddenly he fell for a bitch nearby and would slip off slyly, not come when called, and, if shut up, would whine and pace and send them mad. 'Maybe there's something in this business of having a bitch,' she admitted ruefully. Also, I do deplore the way a dog is constantly lifting a leg and asserting himself. The small inconvenience twice a year when a bitch in on heat is more than compensated for by the pups you may have, or the whole thing can be solved by having her spayed.

I seem to have lost the thread a bit as usual! Anyhow, later that morning a Ceylonese gentleman arrived with a shaggy grey poodle pup in his car. I was entranced and on hearing that it was a bitch, we drove round to the office to see what Leslie thought of her. He came down in his tasting apron and was as keen as I was to have her. The price was astronomical: Rs.450 . . . but she was the only miniature poodle bitch in Ceylon, so we decided to plunge . . . I had visions of making a fortune selling her pups and winning at shows.

Poor Sparkle; she was a dear little dog and it wasn't her fault she was too highly bred. I noticed the same names cropping up on both sides of her pedigree, but thought nothing of it at first. Skipper soon got used to her and she was a gay little soul, tearing about the place, leaping off the leather pouffe and generally brightening things up.

A week or two after we had bought Sparkle, we moved down the road to a house called Shangri-La in Horton Terrace, which had a nice little garden. We were so pleased with it and worked hard in the garden to plant flowers and make it look gay and colourful. We got badly caught, just before the move, by a lugubrious individual who turned up asking for work to help support ten children, he said. We sent him round to the new house to do the garden and after one day, foolishly paid him an advance, 'to get milk for the baby' and never saw him again; I could remember his face for months after.

One day, when we had had Sparkle about two months, she got some sort of skin disease on her back. She used to worry it raw and had to be bandaged. The vet tried various remedies but nothing seemed to help much. Then one awful Friday she became worse. She was unable to lie down for more than a few minutes and then, crying with pain, she would get up and stand pathetically. One hind leg developed a twitch and I had to wake up several times in the night to walk her in the garden, when the twitch would vanish for a short time. She was unable to sleep and I didn't know the vet's home address. On Saturday night she was so restless and pathetic, we took her to the only other vet we knew, who was not actually qualified and was later involved in a court case over a pup he killed. He refused to touch Sparkle, so we just had to wait until Monday. She was unable to sleep for two nights and days; in despair, I tried to rig a sling for her such as sick horses have but it was no good. Like some pitiful grey shadow, she haunted us with twitching limbs and hanging, exhausted head. On Monday we were at the vets by eight o'clock and he gave her an injection to make her sleep. We carried her home in the basket and she slept for three hours. The twitching stopped too but we found she was unable to control herself and slowly, as the injection wore off, the twitch returned. I had asked the vet to put her to sleep that morning but he begged me to try a new medicine for 24 hours, which I did, but only on condition she did not suffer. I had sleeping pills for her in case. By lunchtime, it was obvious she would have to have them; she still couldn't lie down or sleep without. I was very pregnant and terribly upset by the whole affair, and that night we decided she would have to be put to sleep. It was an awful decision to make; she was only a puppy and so sweet, but we really couldn't cope and we hadn't been in Colombo long enough to know that there were in fact, one or two other vets who might have helped.

Next morning I carried her in to the vet, handed her over blindly to the sympathetic vet's assistant, and asked that she should be put out of her misery. Then I fled. We were very subdued that day. No one who has not been through a similar experience can know how painful it is, and the self-questioning that goes on. Did we do enough? Have I given up too easily? I had the same agony as a child in 1946, when Peter, my Yorkshire Terrier, got a bad kidney complaint and had to be put down. I often wonder what will happen to Skipper when she gets too old and sick, but I hope I shall have the courage to have her peacefully put down as soon as she cannot enjoy life or is in pain. I have seen old dogs who have been kept alive by selfish or unthinking owners, and I think our friends deserve better consideration than that after a lifetime of service and love.

I seem to be wallowing in a depressing subject so let's turn from death to life, to the birth of our daughter. I was very confident this time that I knew all the ropes, and one day in early-November I had been having a lot of contractions, so in I went to the hospital. Instantly all contractions ceased and, humiliated, I spent 24 hours lying in bed and was discharged next day and told to come back later. I felt such a fool as we drove back home and all the servants came to greet me! No one had told me that you could have these painless contractions for literally weeks before birth. I pass the information on to those who may benefit!

Eleven days later I went in again. My friends had been very sympathetic and kind, and I can remember relaxing in the cool of Biddy Perkin's air-conditioned bedroom for a morning, for it was very hot. I still swam a lot and did six lengths of the pool the day before Sarah was born. I should like to report that as a result I had an easy delivery, for all my friends had said the second was EASY! In fact it wasn't at all; it was jolly hard work, even though straightforward, and I was pretty tired by the end. She arrived finally at nine o'clock in the evening, looking very over-cooked, with great long nails and dry scaly skin and rather blotchy. All in all, she rather deserved Leslie's query, 'Is she all right? Ought she to look like that?' However, she soon looked better and got fatter and more contented, and was the best behaved of my three babies. Neal was enchanted with her and was always in on a feeding session if he could, with popping eyes, and showed no jealousy for his new sister.

CHAPTER 7

U.K. leave in '59 and we try
our hand at amateur dramatics

THE NEW YEAR, 1959, found us preparing to go on three months' leave in February. As we now had a family, we decided to try living in a hotel, and eventually chose The Park Hill Hotel in Sevenoaks. They sounded friendly and catered specially for overseas people on leave. It was not too far from my parents in London either, or from Leslie's mother in Dulwich.

A few weeks before we left, we went for a walk with Skipper and Neal on some waste land where cows grazed. We were innocently looking at a very new calf curled up asleep some distance away when I was suddenly charged by an irate cow, who presumably thought we had harmful intentions. She caught me a blow with one horn on my thigh before I leapt out of the way, and Leslie jumped in front of her and drove her off. I wish I could say that Skipper rushed at her and saved my life but she kept well out of trouble! I had a vast multicoloured bruise, shaped exactly like a map of Ceylon, which was still there when we got home over a month later!

At the end of February we flew off from Ratmalana airport, Sarah in a carricot, Neal most of the time on the floor at our feet on a pile of blankets, for he wasn't old enough to qualify for a seat. Sarah was marvellous and put up with being fed in all sorts of odd places, including the minute lav., on the plane that roared and vibrated. It was surprising the milk wasn't turned to butter! We had a good flight and everyone was very kind and helpful about the children. We collected a brand new Riley at the airport and drove to Sevenoaks. Mummy and Poppa were there at the hotel to greet us.

The next three months sped hectically by. Life at the Park Hill was never dull and we thoroughly enjoyed it all. Taddy Cook was a large, imposing lady, a wonderful raconteur, with a tall thin husband called Denis. Down the back staircase, which was by our bedroom, we used to hear the most frightful domestic fights, mostly Taddy versus Denis, or Taddy versus Erik the barman and Evelyn the maid. We were astounded and used to hang over the stairs listening for hours fascinated, and it took us several days to realise this was just the usual thing with the Cook family. When we got to know them better, we told them how entertaining it was 'down the back stairs' and Taddy was very tickled.

Just after we arrived at the Park Hill, my sister Ann and her family joined us, on leave from Sierra Leone where her husband worked. It was fun to meet again, this time with our children, although the difference in ages made them rather ill-assorted playmates. Neal was just old enough (twenty-one months) to interfere with the games of Geoff (six) and Amanda (three) and the cry would go up, 'Oh, must she come and spoil it all,' from Amanda, who was having gender trouble at this time! The crowning moment of embarrassment came for her when we put Neal in the bath with her. She covered herself with great modesty and sobbed 'I don't want HER with me.'

In April nothing seemed to go right for us. Ann had to go into hospital to have a plantar wart removed from her foot so Mummy came to stay and look after Geoff and Manda, with a girl to help in the daytime. Mummy got lumbago rather badly at this time and Neal was in bed with a sore throat and cough, which Geoff soon caught. Evelyn's son, John, who slept above the garage with Erik, set fire to his bedclothes one morning, and Taddy thought it was Erik's fault and gave him a terrific bawling out before she discovered it wasn't his fault at all. Manda then went sick and Ann came back from hospital but was still in bed. Here is a part of my diary, written on our fourth wedding anniversary, April 16th:

'What a day for an anniversary! Ann moves upstairs to different room; Manda sick again, Geoff barking, Neal a bit niggly, and on top of it all, doctor finds he can't get Ann's stitches out. Skin's grown over them a bit, so she has to go up to the hospital tomorrow in hired car. Poor Ann, so fed up . . .'

The next day we found Neal had measles . . .

The doctor came and we decided that with so many people in the hotel, it wasn't fair to keep the children there and the doctor said they could go into the isolation hospital near Bromley. Geoff got it the next day and Manda was obviously next, but poor Ann! She felt dreadful; her husband was still in Sierra Leone, so she couldn't discuss it with

Sevenoaks, 1959. Ma, Leslie, Alastair, with Geoff,
Ann with Manda, and myself with Neal.

him; she hoped the children wouldn't be too upset by it. We have a movie film of them all being carried into the ambulance, spots much in evidence! When we got to the hospital, we were surprised to see there were no curtains on the tall windows and the nurse briskly informed up that 'that was all out of date' when we asked, with childhood memories of darkened rooms. Neal was in a huge iron cot in one room, and through a glass panel he could see his cousins next door; they were dressed in an odd assortment of old clothes and we took all their stuff away with us.

Visiting day was only once a week, on Sundays, but as they had been admitted on Saturday, we felt it was a bit soon, so decided to go off and visit friends at Cottenham as we had originally planned. Sarah would not catch measles, I was told, being too young at five months, so she was popped into the carricot and off we went. The first day we were there, Leslie felt ill and next day retired to bed with a high fever. Sarah started a heavy cold. The third day Kate, our hostess, fell ill also, with stomach trouble, and I spent the day sick-nursing! We left on the Thursday, with both invalids more or less recovered, to find our room at the hotel fumigated for us! On Sunday we went with Ann to visit the measly ones, and found Neal didn't recognise us! Geoff and Manda were in an incredible selection of old clothes, Geoff in braces and huge boots, like a Barnardo boy in the old days! He had been most upset that his pyjamas had no elastic in them, just a cord, and that they kept falling down, and he was very shy with the nurses. Anyhow, we were allowed to collect them next day, much to our relief. We were told that the doctor there thought it was only German measles, but this was not so, for later, when Sarah and Tessa caught measles in Ceylon, Neal did not get it.

Apart from all the illnesses, Leslie had a lot of laughs acting as butler at wedding receptions at the hotel and at parties! I also donned a suitable black dress and apron and waited at table at a big lunch, and we had a lot of fun. We used to have wedding receptions at the hotel most Saturdays in the spring, and Leslie would don a black tie and white coat – a regular Jeeves. He used to nip up to our room at intervals and have a cigarette and produce his tips. Once he got half a crown for pulling the plug for someone who couldn't manage it! On one occasion I went out and peered over the banisters at the crowd and caught the butler just toasting a guest with a dry Martini with the aplomb of a bishop! The food at these receptions was superb and little did the guests know that most of the Cook family, plus Erik, Evelyn and any odd guests who could be roped in, had spent the greater part of the night making up marvellous 'short eats' so that they would be fresh.

In May we went down to see Leslie's sister in Cornwall. We took a sleeper and the car also came by train. We stayed at a very smart country club which had just opened, and the whole four days, including fares, set us back about £50, which shattered us a bit!

We also had Sarah's christening in May, with a lovely reception out in the orchard for a few guests, with champagne and the sun shining. As usual, the last few weeks flew past and we were soon saying a reluctant farewell to the Park Hill. How we should miss the fun and games there! Taddy had a succession of unmarried mothers to help in the house and one little girl came after she had had an 'accidental' baby. Taddy said this had happened because the girl thought you couldn't have a baby unless you took all your clothes off first! We wished we'd had a tape to record some of Tad's stories . . .

After an uneventful flight, with the children behaving very well, we were back in Colombo on May 23rd, 1959. It was very hot and humid and we felt the contrast very much. Biddy came round just after we got home and brought Skipper with her. She failed to recognise us really and seemed to have had a wonderful time with the Perkins. She had got on famously with Gilly, the bull terrier. It was nice to be home again with our own things around us, and to catch up on all the news and gossip.

For some time we had been thinking of having another dog, but after the fiasco with poor Sparkle, not a pure-bred one. Not long after we got back from leave, Anne Willis happened to mention that a friend of hers had a young pi-dog she wanted a home for, because she already had a dog and had been landed with the pi-dog by her houseboy. Pam Topen duly came round and brought Pingo with her for me to see. She was about six months old, white with a few lemon markings, a curly tail and lovely brown eyes. Her ears weren't pricked as a pi-dog's often are, but were like a whippet's. I was glad she didn't have the very light, wolf-like eyes that some pi-dogs have, and I liked her very much. She has been with us ever since! I wasn't keen on her name, but somehow it got changed to nothing more inspiring than 'Pingle' or 'Ping'. One of the main reasons that Pam had to find a new home for her was that she had recently chewed a new pair of very expensive child's sandals, but she never did anything like that again so it must have been a last puppy fling. She got rather possessive over me on the first day and sat by me after Pam had left, growling at poor Skip if she came too near, but they were very soon settled down and have been good friends, except for an occasional scrap which is all noise and quite bloodless. Ping is rather a nervous dog in some respects, and though she loves attention, she hates strangers who are too pushing. She likes time to sniff them and sum them up before they pat her. She is very patient with our children, although they have never been allowed to treat her as badly as some poor beasts are. You know the kind of thing: 'He's marvellous, the children can do ANYTHING with him and he puts up with it.' To my mind, it is very wrong to bring up a child to think it can do what it likes with any animal, and it is a pathetic sight to watch a patient, long-suffering dog put up with being mauled unmercifully. There is also the possibility that one day the worm will turn and it will give a jolly good nip, when it will then doubtless be put down as vicious instead of being congratulated.

Not long after we got Pingle, I found a vast number of ticks on Skipper. These are horrible pests that bury their head in the dog's skin and suck the blood; they can cause tick fever. I rushed to the vet and he gave me a new powder to dilute with water for a bath. It was a continental preparation and the directions were in litres, kilogrammes or something, and he had to work out the amounts in teaspoonfuls and pints. Eventually he gave me a small package and said it should go with a pint of water. I rushed home and soaked her in it, afterwards sitting back expectantly to see the ticks fall off. After two hours they were still there alive, so I couldn't bear it any more and set to work with my eyebrow tweezers and some disinfectant to pull them off. A few hours later Skipper became very ill. She was sick, had diarrhoea, and kept crying with pain. I rang the vet and he recommended nux vomica in brandy every 15 minutes. I dosed her from 7.15 to 10.00 when she seemed a little better, but she still cried at intervals and shivered a lot. I thought she had licked some of the disinfectant I had used and it was years later that I used the same powder, this time in a small packet with full directions on it. I found that the amount of powder I had used to a pint was about ten times the normal dose, and there was a warning about exceeding the quantities on the packet, with an antidote given. Skip had had a very narrow escape and it was two days before she was back to normal again.

The night all this happened we were supposed to be going to a social given by a local amateur dramatics group that Anne Willis belonged to. She was a keen member, having studied Drama and Speech Training in London in her youth. The group was having a membership drive and she wanted Leslie and me to join. I had done quite a lot of acting at school, where we were lucky in having Miss Viola Compton (Fay Compton and Compton MacKenzie's sister) as our teacher. She was brilliant and we used to sweep the board at the local drama festivals. Leslie's acting had been confined to a rather lighthearted effort as a butler during his time in the RAF, and he wasn't very keen to do any more. However, I felt he needed something to do in his spare time to stop him agonising about the office. He is the conscientious type who sits at home and worries about tea matters.

We eventually went along to the group's next meeting and we joined in, reading one-act plays, meeting people and chatting, and in the end we joined. I paid for Leslie, to clinch the matter, for he was still not over keen, something we laughed at in years to come when he had been in most of the group's plays.

We had just joined the group when we heard that the other amateur drama club in Colombo was looking for someone to play the leading lady in *Dial M for Murder*. A friend of mine knew the producer and for some reason felt I might suit the part, and he got in touch with me and arranged an audition. The idea thrilled me to bits and I read for the part and was offered it, much to my delight. It was the part taken by Grace Kelly in the film, and though long, was very rewarding. However, one of the strings attached was that I should join the club. I wrote saying we had just joined one drama club and didn't really want to join another. Was there any sort of temporary membership, I asked? I was told 'no', so I sent a cheque rather reluctantly, and was therefore shattered to receive a letter a few days later telling me that rather than accept my reluctant membership, they were returning my cheque and would not be needing me for the part . . . We had been rehearsing for almost a month by then. I knew most of my part, and the first night was only two weeks away, so you can imagine my feelings! There was a certain amount of healthy rivalry between the two groups, though many people belonged to both, but feelings ran pretty high on both sides for a time. Anyhow, they say it's an ill wind that blows nobody any good (it was years before I worked out the meaning of this particular saw!) and within ten days we were attending the audition of our own group's production of *See How They Run*, which Anne Willis was producing. This was a roaring farce, very different from the Group's usual efforts, for they had the reputation of being rather highbrow. When we joined the International Theatre Group, it had just acquired a new President, who was determined to put the group on its feet. We had only thirty members, and most of those only met when there was a show on. Some were only 'ticket members', i.e. those who only wanted the complimentary tickets issued to members for their shows. Fred Staddon, the new President, felt strongly that the group needed some sort of social contact to keep members in touch, so he instituted the Maggi. This name was derived from the initials Meet and Greet Evening, and used to be held monthly at different members' houses. There we ran an illicit bar, read plays, listened to records, had lectures on theatrical subjects or just chatted. They were a great success but one could never be sure about how many would turn up. At the

Myself as the Vicar's wife, Leslie as the Bishop, Barry Whittington as an impostor vicar. Our first effort at amateur dramatics, See How They Run, *Colombo, 1959, with the International Theatre Group.*

smallest Maggi we had there were about six, which was no less fun than the ones where we had forty or so. The group was pretty low in funds and Fred decided we must recoup with a really low farce, so *See How They Run* was chosen. It was a hysterically nonsensical romp about a country vicar and his glamorous wife, with lots of mix-ups of identity and the vicar losing his trousers. No one pretended it was high-class dramatic fare, but how we all enjoyed ourselves – and that included the audience! There are always two different opinions about amateur acting. some feel they should stick to 'easy' things like farce and not poach on the professionals' territory, but others liked a play with a little more to it. We never did please everyone, of course, and in the course of a year we used to try and do a thriller, a comedy and a straight play.

We were both very lucky in our first parts, for I was cast as the Vicar's carefree, scatty wife, who scandalised the locals by wearing slacks (this was during the war) and Leslie was my uncle, the Bishop, who got involved with an escaped prisoner-of-war and batty curates. Up to this time the sets and scenery used to be done by one man, who was paid for his services. This time, he was unable to do it unaided, so members who were good at carpentry and painting set to work and did the job just as well, thereby saving money. I helped do a large backdrop of a garden scene, which took me back to the old days at school, when we used to paint our own scenery.

I had a vast part to learn and was on stage nearly all the time. Rehearsals were pretty hysterical at first, because we thought we were so funny. Leslie and the vicar used to have one particular Achilles' heel, a not at all funny bit of dialogue, which for some mysterious reason they were unable to finish without giggling. They used to retire to a secluded spot backstage and solemnly go through the dialogue: 'I am the Bishop of Lax, who are you?' 'But *I*, sir, am the Bishop of Lax!' and then off they'd go, like a pair of schoolgirls in spite of all the good intentions. We used to get terribly hot at rehearsals because of all the dashing about; it was the sort of play where someone was always coming or going. There were three doors and a French window, all used.

We were most excited by the pre-publicity in the papers. At that time Ceylon had one morning paper and two evening ones, and they all gave pictures and articles about us. I had my picture in, with a write-up about my past, which had been gathered in a special interview at home by a charming lady reporter! We had six weeks' rehearsal for most of our shows, the last two usually being in the theatre in the evenings, when the set builders and painters knocked off. For this show we moved into the theatre on Sept. 23rd, 1959 and the first night was to be October 2nd. On Sept. 25th the cook came to me in the morning in great excitement, saying that the Prime Minister, Mr Bandaranaike, had been shot at his home, which was only half a mile away. It was a sad and ironic fact that the assassin was a Buddhist monk and to a Buddhist all life is sacred. The bhikkus, as the monks are called, were very active in Ceylon politics. On one occasion, in the course of a dispute, they all sat down in the Prime Minister's garden until he acceded to their wishes; they were a powerful faction indeed.

The next day Mr Bandaranaike died of his terrible wounds. It was amazing he had lived so long; we had all the details of his shattered liver, spleen and caecum, and also the news that his assailant had been shot in a very embarrassing place but was expected to live. The body

lay in state at his house for two days before being moved to the House
of Representatives. The queues to pay their last respects stretched for
miles, and some waited eleven hours in all weathers. It was very odd,
for during his life Mr B. had been something of a joke to many. If he
appeared on the news at the cinema, the local inhabitants would roar
with laughter at him, but after his death he became a martyr and
everyone was suddenly full of praise for him. I went out one night
with the dogs and found the queue all the way down the road, but
they were in a holiday mood and I got so 'chi-iked' with my brief
shorts that I cut short the dogs' walk in a hurry. They are a very
emotional people, the Ceylonese, and are as quick to tears as to anger.
Ceylon has one of the highest murder rates in the world, more than
one a day, and yet they are mostly very kind, cheerful people!

All this excitement meant we had to postpone our first night at least
until after the funeral, so we decided to open on Tuesday, Oct. 6th, thus
giving ourselves a little extra time to get used to the set, lights and
costumes. We all rushed into town daily to see how the advance
bookings were going, and it looked quite good. People were happy to
escape from the troubles of the world for a couple of hours, and after a
fairly good dress rehearsal, we were ready for the real thing! Our main
worry was how to cope with laughs – always supposing we had any. It
is the greatest mark of an amateur that he doesn't wait for laughter to
die down before he speaks and nothing is more irritating than to lose
half the dialogue in this way. We had a small invited audience from the
Navy on the dress rehearsal night, which helped a lot, but we were
astounded on the night at the howls of laughter that greeted our
antics. It was simply wonderful. At one point I had to faint, and lying
there on the dusty boards, listening to the waves of laughter at some
comedy business between the bishop and the vicar, was an experience
I shall always remember. We all felt pretty limp after but most jubilant,
and next day we were thrilled by some excellent reviews. I have
described this all in detail because it was the first of 13 full-length and
seven one-act plays that either Leslie or I acted in over the next five
years. It was the most rewarding hobby we ever took up. It was hard
work, often frustrating, but what fun we had! I may say that we did not
have fun at the customers' expense. Our standards were very high
indeed, and I have seen things done in the professional theatre, small
careless details, which we, as amateurs, would never have done. I later

saw a professional production of a play we were once both in and it wasn't a patch on our show; they played for cheap laughs and didn't even bother to change the clothes of one character in spite of a passage of time in the plot.

As a result of our acting, we made dozens of new friends too and one even had the fun of people who were strangers coming up and saying nice things about 'your show', or ringing you up to say they didn't agree with the critic in the paper. The critics were sometimes a thorn in our side. We sent the papers free tickets for the first night, but all too often it looked as if whoever was sent didn't want the job, and anyhow knew nothing about drama. Some would make nasty personal remarks, and I have read two really vitriolic reviews (not of our shows) that should never have been printed. I suppose we share this burden with the professional actors, and it made us appreciate the really conscientious reviewers who offered genuine constructive criticism and really appreciated the work and general set-up of an amateur group. I remember once, we did *Five Finger Exercise*, which had a fabulous set on three levels. The ground floor was a sitting room, then a staircase and landing, then another staircase up to an upper bedroom. We made the whole thing ourselves, out of tractor packing-cases, for a very small sum, and most critics raved about it. However, one gentleman wrote; 'The sets, which were adequate, could have been better.' You can imagine our feelings! However, it all added to the excitement of life, I suppose.

See How They Run ran for six hectic nights and made the I.T.G. a profit. Most nights something untoward happened, but we found out that mostly our audience was unaware of all the slips and missed lines. There weren't that number of them and of course we were hypersensitive to what went on, but mostly they passed undetected. On dress rehearsal night I had missed an entry. I stood by the door off-stage, idly listening to the bishop and the maid chatting, when I suddenly realised they were not sticking to the book!

'Yes, I expect Penelope will be here SOON,' said the bishop loudly. 'She should be here any moment NOW,' and I shot on, scarlet with embarrassment to save the poor things any more ad-libbing. It did mean, however, that I never missed that cue again! Most people were very good at covering up for someone who had 'run dry' and in their terror couldn't hear the whispered prompt. I think the most ghastly moment any I.T.G. member had was during a sequel to *See How They Run* called *Pool's Paradise*. This time Leslie was the vicar and was busy chatting to his wife, having asked the maid to bring him a cup of coffee. The maid, listening for her cue to re-enter, suddenly realised that the vicar had skipped a whole page and was shortly coming up for a completely different cue for the maid to enter, this time from upstairs carrying a hot water bottle. This was a Moment of Truth for the wretched April, but she was a resourceful type and taking a lightning decision, tore up the back stairs and just entered, slightly breathless, with the coffee. Mercifully, Leslie hadn't even realised what he'd done, or he might have complicated matters even more by trying to put back the part he'd left out. It is at times like this that you wonder why you act. My ghastly moment came in a one-act play. We were gathered round the death-bed of my husband. In a feeble voice, he said to me, 'Mary, fetch my little black book from the wardrobe,' but then added in a bloodchilling whisper, '*I don't think it's there*' and closed his eyes and lay back, leaving me to totter to the wardrobe, where the stage manager, bless him, was standing off stage just by it, ready to hand me the book. As if this wasn't enough, a bit later the dying man asked for a glass of water and again helpfully added *sotto voce* that it wasn't there. Again I crossed the stage to the alert s.m., who had noticed the deficit and again handed me the glass . . . We didn't often slip up so badly on details. Another time a maid, who had removed her shoes for quietness backstage, forgot to put them on and wheeled on a tea trolley bare-footed! Other members were notorious for forgetting lines and we used to be in a ferment watching the poor prompt almost on stage, following every line with a finger ready to hiss helpfully if needed. Prompt was a beastly job. You had to know the play backwards, and it was too easy to jump in with a quick prompt, only to realise that you had just ruined a beautifully timed pregnant pause, carefully planned by the actor concerned!

There was a wonderful 'togetherness' about being in a play, and we all used to have a lot of fun recalling old shows. When we first joined, we used to listen enviously to the old hands reminiscing and wish we could join in, but very soon we were able to. Of course, you did get the odd rows and petty jealousies, and even a spot of adultery, which livened everything up a lot, but there was surprisingly little temperament.

After a play was over, we used to have a party and the next morning we would all gather to break up the set. It was perfectly beastly to have to tear down all our hard work, but we made our flats of dexion and hardboard, so they could be used again and again until they fell to bits. It took so little time to demolish compared with the labour of putting it up. After it was all over, we used to feel terribly flat and sat at home reminiscing and planning the next show.

I hope I haven't run on too much about our dramatics, but they were such an important part of our life for five years that I had to deal with it rather fully. Later Skipper was to be involved in a play. So it isn't too irrelevant to this story if I seem to talk a lot about the I.T.G.

CHAPTER 8

Holidays, hens and pups

As SOON AS WE HAD FINISHED *See How They Run*, we started planning the next production. The Council decided on a thriller and, after reading several suitable plays, chose Agatha Christie's *Ten Little Niggers*. Although many Ceylonese have dark skins, nobody thought we ought to change the title, but I notice that when the film came to Kenya recently, it was called *Ten Little Indians*. We both attended the audition and Leslie got the part of the old general, who was murdered fairly early in the play. I got the job of décor, which meant I had to choose the paint, curtains and loose covers for the set. It was an awfully hard job, as one really couldn't tell if all was well until it was done, by which time it was too late to alter anything but the smallest details. Rehearsals started again, with Anne Willis's husband George as producer, and we were glad to be back in harness once more.

1959 drew to a close uneventfully, except that I got very tight for the first, and I hope the last, time in my life. We were at the Perkins' for a cocktail party for our visiting Chairman. I had two or three of John's enormous whiskys, and had got to the harmless but giggly stage when we left. Unfortunately we 'went on' and I stupidly disregarded the warnings that I had had enough (I can always tell, my tongue feels too big for my mouth, an odd sensation!) and had two more whiskys. It was awful; we went on to the Otters Club and I have dim memories of trying to play billiards and eating very hot prawns. I spent most of the time tottering back and forth to and from the loo, and Ginny Godwin got a bit anxious and kept an eye on me. Then some bright person suggested we 'went on' again, this time to the Queen's Club, a very august place. I was walking downstairs with Bryan Patt, whose wife was away in the U.K. at the time. Bryan had just had an accident in his car and had a broken arm in plaster, stuck out at an odd angle on a frame. It was rather a case of the blind leading the blind, and finally, when we reached our car, things got a bit confused and I found myself lying flat on my back in a flowerbed with Bryan hovering over me giggling like a maniac. Somehow he and Leslie got me into the car and we went to the Queen's. I made a disreputable picture, with earth all down the back of my dress and carrying my high-heeled shoes, which I was quite unable to wear. Ginny escorted me straight to the ladies and I lay thankfully on a couch there until Leslie took me home. I had to be supported up the path and was later very sick. Next morning I did get up, but after two minutes retired to bed, both sadder and wiser. I have never done anything so silly since. It was a horrible lesson, like being in a different person's skin. However, it had repercussions. Lipton's had a new bachelor, just out from London. He viewed my behaviour, quite rightly, with horror, but no one could persuade him that I wasn't a habitual drunkard. As Bryan and I made our unsteady descent to the car, he said to Claude Godwin, 'I feel jolly sorry for that chap Pierson.' Claude, mystified, asked why, and was told, 'Well, having a wife like that – awful.' Claude tried to redeem my good name but the young man wouldn't believe him. Not long after he amazed us all by leaving the company. He hated Ceylon and thought everyone drank too much. Poor Biddy Perkins, who was the most conscientious boss's wife that I know, was most upset and I had to assure her she had not neglected him at all.

Early in 1960 I started to keep hens again. During the War we had them, and I liked their personalities. Furthermore, it was wonderful to have fresh eggs. I had a very nice cook then, named John, who asked me one day if I wanted any hens as his wife up-country kept a lot. After due discussion with Leslie, who said firmly 'God, no, not hens,' I gave John a week's leave and he promised to return with a selection of Leghorns and a breed that was new to me and sounded like 'Ariars'. I afterwards worked out it was 'R.I.R.'s' (Rhode Island Reds!). Days passed and I put in the finishing touches to a house John and I had made. It was of bricks, bought cheaply from a house up the road that was being demolished. Poor Leslie – it was the last straw to be asked to carry bricks in the boot of the car! John and I worked like mad. He had a fish-slice and I had a trowel, and we made a pretty good job of it, with a cement floor and a large green-painted door. It was while I was making this door one day in the front porch that an American lady came to the gate. She said she was a Jehovah's Witness and showed imminent signs of bringing out her literature, so I said hastily, 'I'm afraid your seed will fall on barren ground here,' (rather aptly put, I thought) and I went on to explain that I had already had a nasty experience in Calcutta with one of her colleagues. It had happened when I was at the Animal Clinic, sitting at the desk answering the phone and writing letters. An American lady was shown in and sitting down, brightly greeted me and produced out of her sling bag a large Bible. Before I could utter a word, she read me a long extract and went on to give a sermon about the coming of the End. Was I ready? she asked. I have never been so uncomfortable and I had an awful job to get rid of her. I wonder why I find religion outside church so embarrassing? I don't mean an informal discussion, but being prayed over in bed, for instance, makes me shrivel up inside. It has happened to me three times, once when I was a student in bed with chickenpox, and twice in the nursing home after having babies. I wish this wasn't so, for it is a nice idea and why shouldn't one pray outside a church? I do, but always to myself. I think perhaps a lot depends on the person who is praying. One padre got terribly bogged down in a very long prayer, and it's hard to concentrate when one is lying in bed in a shortie nightie suffering from piles . . .

As usual, I'm off the track again; I told the lady at the gate about her too-zealous comrade in Calcutta and she was very good and didn't press me any more. I have the greatest admiration for people who can go from house to house, stand on street corners and generally get rebuffed by passers by, but I could never have the incredible strength to deny my child a blood transfusion, as some do, whatever the Bible says. After all, it is written by men and has been translated, so it must be hard to know how much to believe.

My hen-house was finished, fresh sawdust was on the floor, the nest-boxes filled with straw ready for all the eggs. All I needed was the hens, but no John arrived. Eventually he came back two days late and I was unable really to scold him because the hens were a gift! At last a taxi arrived and John jumped out and removed a small box from the roof. We carried it into the hen-run and opened it to reveal an odd selection of four fowls. One was black, one brown, one white with a top-knot, and one small scrawny brown one that later revealed himself as a cockerel! The brown and the black did look as if they were ready to lay. Their combs were large and red and six days later they *both* laid their first eggs after much palaver. A few days later, the brown one decided a box wasn't good enough and I found her in the spare bedroom in the cupboard. I shooed her out. She had come in via the window, which looked out on to the run and the next thing I knew, she was next-door in our room, standing doubtfully on the bedside table!

As well as doing décor for the play, I also designed the programme cover. This was great fun, but one was a little limited in the design because it was to be printed, so there could not be too much detail. However, in the end I did a huge negro face wearing a frightened expression, and round it scattered various objects from the rhyme: a bee, an axe, a noose, a bear and a handsome red herring. It was a most odd sensation to see the finished product as a cover for two hundred and fifty programmes!

In February we decided to take our first holiday and Ginny Godwin said she would have the children and Joslin. We took them round the night before, as we planned to leave early next morning. One often thinks how much one would like a holiday from the children, but we certainly felt very odd indeed that evening without them.

We left home just before eight the next morning; we had booked for one of the Reserves at Yala, Buttuwa, where you took your own food, water and bedding. We had done 25 miles when Leslie realised he had left all the entry permits and papers behind at the house . . . That set us back rather, and tempers were not improved by an appalling lunch at Galle. There were no potatoes, the ice cream was melted, the soup watery and the fish half raw. In disgust, Leslie put a five-rupee note on the table and walked out! We spent that night at the rest-house at Hambantota, just by the sea. Leonard Woolf, the author, was there, and we watched a party given for him and dined ourselves on delicious fried prawns.

Next morning, we bought bread and potatoes and other last-minute supplies and set off on the last leg to Yala. After Tissa, the road was very bad and it clouded over and began to rain. We arrived at the main office at midday and picked up a ranger, who then guided us to Buttuwa bungalow. On the way we saw spotted deer and wild pig. The bungalow was right by the sea, surrounded by a rocky outcrop and near a small waterhole. The actual building was just a tin-roofed shack; one large room did as sitting and dining room, and off it was a small kitchen, with a kerosene cooker and a cook to work it! The bedroom was one long room with four beds in it. There was an outside lavatory, but it had a plug! When we arrived, there was an elephant standing near the bungalow, an unexpected and exciting welcome. He had only half a tail and was a well-known visitor called Buttuwa Bill. Ceylon elephants are just like Indian ones and you can't really believe they aren't from a circus or zoo. When you see African ones, they really look wild, but the Asian variety are so frequently seen in captivity that they look docile.

We passed an extremely uncomfortable night. It poured with rain and the roof leaked. Leslie reckoned that we might have to leave next morning in case the roads got too muddy to move later. We went to bed early and were careful not to tread on the tiny frogs that hopped about the floor. Mosquitoes plagued us and we had no nets. Finally I found two bed-bugs and then we just started to laugh! Things couldn't have been any worse so we just pulled the sheets over our faces and went to sleep.

We were woken at daybreak by the ranger, who whispered there were two elephants outside. We sat up in bed and watched them. They were standing quietly, caressing each other with their trunks in a most touching way. Then they wandered off and we had a cup of excellent coffee and set out in the car to look for more game. It was fine and warm now, but the ground was wet and soon we got bogged down while watching some birds at a waterhole. Amarasena, the tracker, nobly set off to get help, and we sat and watched an enchanting selection of storks and waders. He returned after twenty minutes with two men, but even then we were still stuck, so he went off again and brought back three more. Still we remained firmly stuck and then, luckily, a jeep appeared with a couple in it we knew from I.T.G. meetings. They were staying at Yala bungalow and their extra strength finally got us out! We were most grateful and drove back carefully to a late breakfast. We saw more elephants, peafowl, jungle cock and masses of other birds, which I looked up in my book. In the afternoon we went on the beach and later Leonard Woolf turned up to see the place, and I was able to tell the senior ranger with him about the bed-bugs, which I felt was a form of wild life that was unwelcome even here!

In the evening the cook produced mosquito nets (why not last night for goodness sake?) and after a peaceful evening sitting on the veranda with a hissing power lamp, we passed a peaceful night; it was dry enough to sleep on the veranda and much cooler. I woke up once in the night to see the dim form of a big Sambhur stag passing nearby, and in the morning I found his slot-marks in the sand.

Next morning we went to Yala bungalow, which was by a river, and were shown the pug-marks of a leopard very near the house. We spent the afternoon on the beach, and on the way back, going over the rocks, found an elephant fifteen feet below us! We watched him for some time, then crept back home. The birds were simply glorious. I recorded 33 new species I had never seen, and we also saw buffalo, crocodile, jackal, hare, turtle, mongoose, rock squirrel and talagoya, the latter being a large kind of monitor lizard about three feet long. That afternoon, the cook brought me a tiny leveret he had found in the grass. It was just like an English one I had once reared. I reluctantly let it go outside and it hopped composedly away.

Next morning we were most reluctant to leave the peace and beauty we had found, but the blow was softened by the arrival of the next tenants at 7.45, with their transistor radios and loud voices. On the way out we saw more elephants, making a total of 16 adults and 6 youngsters for our stay.

We went home a different way, and this time had a good but plain lunch at Ratnapura rest-house. It cost only 4/9d each for roast beef, soup and fruit salad.

We arrived home in time for tea and found our precious front lawn looking like a bomb crater. In our absence, we had arranged for the water-pipes to be cleaned as the flow was down to a rusty trickle. They had also knocked out a lot of the pantry floor, but at least when the job was done, the supply improved.

Next morning, we went to the Godwins and collected the children, who were very glad to see us and had apparently behaved well in our absence. We were very glad to be home, but we missed the calm and the leisurely pace of Buttawa, with no newspapers, wireless, phones or even lights that switched on!

Rehearsals for *Ten Little Niggers* continued, but not very frequently, as we still had plenty of time. Leslie was therefore able to have a few more days of his local leave and we spent them up on Dambatenne, Lipton's tea estate and Thomas Lipton's pride in the old days. This time we were able to take the children and were to stay in the Assistant Manager's bungalow as he was on leave. We had a lot of rain and fog as we climbed upwards along winding roads, the air becoming cooler and damper. We stopped for lunch at Beli Huloya, a nice rest-house on the edge of a rushing stream which tore through rocks and gorges and made a great noise.

We arrived at Dambatenne about teatime and found the bungalow small but cosy. It seemed odd to have blankets on the beds, but you certainly needed them. We saw there were nets, but didn't use them until later in the evening, when we went to look at Neal as he slept and saw he was covered in mozzies! Somehow, at that height we had felt there would be fewer of these pests.

Dambatenne was run in those days by Chris Power and after we arrived, his wife Ann rang me to say hello and arranged to meet next morning. John Perkins was also there on a visit, so Ann and I had coffee whilst the men went off to see the estate.

Dambatenne is a show-place and has a superb garden. The great lawn slopes down to a sheer drop of a thousand feet. You are 5,000 feet up anyway and on a clear day you can see the sea at Hambantota, 75 miles away. The garden is full of wonderful flowers: roses abound and also tall hibiscus trees, which in Colombo are usually only bushes. Ann took us all round the grounds, the swimming pool, the little summer-house on the hillside that Lipton had made, her ducks and hens, the pet monkey and the house itself. It was vast and rambling, with a fireplace in every room and a big sitting room that looked out on to the view. There was another sitting room as well, so there was no lack of space for the children to play.

In the evening we had dinner with the Powers and it was just like home: candles in silver candlesticks, the fire flickering, the cool air.

The next morning Chris drove us over the estate in a Land Rover. Some of the roads were just tracks, with a sheer drop on one side, and they twisted about in impossible looking hairpin bends, so acute that often you couldn't drive straight round without backing first. We also dropped into the maternity home and to Leslie's horror, only just missed the birth of a baby by ten minutes! The estate had its own schools, housing, temples and dispensary, and was like a small independent country; some of the workers live there and die there without travelling very far away from home. Chris then took us to one of the schools, and we felt slightly embarrassed when faced with the stares of thirty or so infants clutching slates, rather like a royal visit!

The next day we had a pleasant drive in sunny weather into nearby

Bandarawela. It was amazing up there. One moment it would be bright and fine, then down would come the rain or a blanket of fog would descend. It was hard to know how to dress. We also visited the factory and I was amazed at the work that goes into making a cup of tea. That evening I heard Leslie's lines, for we were leaving next day and after missing some rehearsals, he had to be word perfect. He always finds it an uphill job, and far easier to let the lines 'gel' once he is on-stage and is helped with the moves, but this is not very fair on others who are managing without the book. It is a major bereavement to some actors, the day they cast away the book and launch themselves without it. Lines that you knew perfectly in the bath earlier just vanish, and you are left groping feebly, murmuring excuses to the wretched producer. Some players have to be forced to give up their books; they try and secrete them in useful places. We have had some hilarious evenings reading *Coarse Acting* by Michael Green and I recommend it to anyone interested in drama! He has a lot to say about the actor who has lines trouble, all of it funny.

We left Dambatenne next morning and had an uneventful journey home, where we saw in the papers the news of Princess Margaret's engagement to Tony Armstrong-Jones. I also found that one baby budgie had hatched in the aviary in the garden. It was hideous but it was my first one in spite of many eggs that were laid. The baby did well for two weeks although one leg seemed to be a bit crooked. Then one afternoon I looked inside the box and found it dead, it's skull gashed. The murderer was plainly a spinster hen budgie, for she had blood on her beak and hovered around the box. I presume jealousy was the reason but I was very upset and that night I dazzled the murderer by torchlight and put her in a small cage. Next day I presented her to a friend who had an aviary. 'Lovebirds' is certainly a misnomer, especially in this case, and if you have ever tried to handle a budgie, you will know that unless it is finger tame, it will bite severely; I always used a scarf to protect my hand.

I found the hens very frustrating; the two main layers often both went broody and stopped laying, but when they did lay, it was marvellous to have the fresh eggs. I decided to buy three White Leghorns, a breed we had kept before and which do not go broody. I ordered three from an up-country farm and told John reluctantly that Tatty must go. This was the odd brown bird that soon turned out to be a cockerel. When my lovely snowy Leghorn pullets arrived, Tatty became very masculine and essayed his first crow. Poor John looked uncomfortable and said apologetically, 'I doesn't like to cut that bird.' I hastily asked if he knew anyone who might like Tatty and he said he had a friend who duly arrived next day and carried him off – the right way up, as I was relieved to see.

Our First Night drew near; I spent a lot of time working on the set. One thing that took a long time was a large copy of the 'Ten Little Niggers' rhyme that hung above the mantlepiece. It was great fun to do. I used a thick printing nib and a piece of paper about a foot and a half wide and nearly three feet long. There was also a backdrop of sea and a wall which I did with each brick individually shaded. There were six rows, each with fifty-two bricks, so you can imagine my feelings when I finally sat down in the auditorium to view my work, only to find you couldn't see more than about ten bricks at a time from any seat!

The play went off well and once more we made a profit. The set I had had misgivings about, for it was a 'modern' one, circa 1938. I think it looked quite attractive. No one did anything too awful, except one night when the electrician (nothing to do with the I.T.G., but provided by the theatre) forgot the most important spotlight of the whole play, at that dramatic moment when, after a blackout, someone lights a candle and a spotlight shows the judge with a bullet hole through his forehead sitting in the window seat. We had awful trouble getting that bullet hole to show up. Ordinary red was no good, and in the end, almost-black proved the best.

We had another holiday at Easter and this time went to Galle. In the old days it was a Portuguese fort and it still has huge walls and battlements looking out onto the sea. Some of the streets are very narrow and the old houses have half-doors like stables. Altogether it is a very picturesque place.

According to my diary, we left Sarah at home with Joslin and only spent two nights away. As soon as we got back, all my new pullets began to lay, all within four days – I was so pleased!

In May Ping came into season and we had an awful time with all the dogs who came round. One in particular was a large black and white pi with prick ears and a curly tail. He was the bane of my life and leapt over our low wall repeatedly. One evening we were in the middle of supper when I heard a yelp from the garden. I rushed out to find the happy couple *in flagrante delicto* by the gate . . . It was too late to do anything, so we left them in disgust and went back to our meal, speculating what the pups would be like. Ping came back ten minutes later absolutely grovelling. She crept up to us and her lop-sided grin appeared, as it always does when she is in trouble. It was really very funny as we hadn't scolded her, but she knew somehow that she wasn't very popular!

Once the deed was done, we accepted her pregnancy with a good grace and she had extra food and vitamins. Her waistline expanded according to plan and in the last week or two we could see the pups kicking about, which fascinated the children. I have never been a believer in telling children nonsense about storks and gooseberry bushes, and this was a practical demonstration for them. I had marked The Day in my diary, July 12th, but I was surprised to find how prompt she was. After breakfast, right on the day, she began to pant and wander about whining, stopping sometimes when a contraction came. I had arranged a bed for her in the lavatory in a roomy box and we went in there, and I consoled her, for she was very restless, and kept putting a paw out to me asking for help. They say bitches are best left alone but she was very plainly glad of my presence. Only an hour after the first symptoms, the first pup was born, very easily, and I was most impressed at the new mother's efficiency; she bit the cord, tore off the sac that enclosed the pup, ate the afterbirth and washed the squirming baby. It was a dog and I was glad, for I had reluctantly decided that any bitches must be put to sleep. It would be hard enough to find good homes for the dogs, being only pi, but a bitch would be impossible. My doctor had given me the remains of a bottle of chloroform when I told him why I wanted it, for I feel that drowning is a cruel and revolting death, whatever some people may say. Half an hour later another little dog was born, and by now Ping knew exactly what it was about and coped splendidly. Two more came at half hour intervals, and the last was a bitch. I was thankful there was only one, but although I hated to take so new a life, I felt it was preferable to giving her away later to a poor home. I took her away from Pingle unnoticed and put her in a small box with a pad of cottonwool soaked in the chloroform and left her for an hour. When I took her out and buried her, she looked peaceful and was lying as I had left her in the box. Meanwhile

Neal, Sarah, Skip and prostrate mother Ping with her puppies,
Colombo, January, 1963.

Pingle settled down with her squeaking, wriggling family. She was a devoted mother and no one but I was allowed to touch the pups. I let the children look from a distance, but I could see Ping was tense and didn't like it. Poor Skipper tried to have a look, hearing the squeaks, and was amazed at the rude behaviour of her friend. I was most surprised at the clean, unfussy way the pups had been born. It was a wonderful experience to see it all and I was very touched at Ping's trust in me. If I picked up a pup, she would gaze up at it, ears pricked and a most wonderful expression of love on her face, until I put it back. She had to be led out for exercise and couldn't wait to get back. Of course, as the pups grew, her concern wore off a little and by the time they were about five weeks old she was a wee bit tired of them, though until then she had been a model parent. As the pups grew fatter, she grew more and more like a skeleton in spite of three meals a day and extra milk and meat!

The pups were all black and white. One was larger than the rest and had longer fur, and we called him Chubby. Another had a large black patch over his eye, so he was Shiner, and the smallest, who had a lot of black on him, was Little Willie. Poor Skipper! She hated her role as auntie. They mauled her and pulled her beard and tail and generally showed no respect for her, even though she growled thunderously at them. Once they were able to stagger about fairly steadily, I took them out in the garden. Their newly found confidence vanished immediately, and they crept about pathetically, tummies on the ground and tails at half-mast, crying for the familiar surroundings of the bathroom again. After a time, of course, they got used to the wide world of the garden and used to rush about and charge higgledy-piggledy up the veranda steps into the house. Chubby gave me a nasty time one day when I saw his hind legs sticking out of a storm-drain that went under the veranda steps. I caught hold of his legs and tail and pulled, but to my horror he pulled against me and began to vanish . . . the drain turned a corner at right-angles after the first six inches and I knew he would only reach a dead end if he went in any further. At the risk of hurting him, I took a firm grip and pulled hard and out he popped, very indignant at his rest being disturbed!

Finally, when they were six weeks old, we sent them off to various homes I had found. Two went to the Deaf and Blind School and one went to a priest on the outskirts of Colombo. It was very quiet after they had gone, but I think both Ping and Skip revelled in the peace!

CHAPTER 9

Arab horses, more plays
and more pups!

NOT LONG AFTER WE HAD got rid of the puppies, I achieved one of
my most cherished ambitions: to ride an Arab stallion. I had first
seen an Arab at a horse show when I was in my early teens. I was
completely bowled over by the beauty of these marvellous horses, and
immediately began writing off to all the breeders for stud-cards and
photographs. Looking back, I am amazed at the generosity and
patience of my patrons, for although some never replied (and even kept
the stamp I sent), many were incredibly generous and sent me
wonderful photos of their animals. One kind gentleman even sent me
Lady Wentworth's large book, *The Authentic Arabian Horse*, saying he
regretted he could only lend it to me. I was most touched at his
generosity and carefully packed it up and sent it back when I had read
it. Many breeders seemed to think I was in the business and advised
me to send my mares NOW as it was late in the year; how I wished I
had even one to send! At one show I went to, accompanied by a great
friend, Pen and my father, there was a class for mares with foals at foot.
Pen and I were admiring a chestnut mare being groomed for this class
with her frisky foal, when the man turned to us and said he was short-
handed and would one of us like to lead the foal into the ring. We
were paralysed with excitement but had sufficient wit to draw lots and
I won. Poppa was most astonished to see his daughter in the ring
leading a foal, but he took two photos of us. We didn't even reach the
front line but even so, it was the nicest thing that had happened to me
for a long time. We followed the colt's career. He was later christened
'Anzar', but after some time we lost touch.

To anyone who doesn't know about Arabs, it is hard to describe the
impact they make. They are not large but the stallions especially are
bursting with life and energy as they toss their wonderful manes and
flirt their great uncut tails, for an Arab's mane and tail are never cut or
pulled like a thoroughbred's, and sometimes the forelock sweeps down

to the nostrils and the tail almost touches the ground. They have great big eyes, pointed ears, and wonderful delicate faces with the 'dished' or concave profile. I always feel that after seeing an Arab, no other horse can quite stir me, with the possible exception of a Shire or Clydesdale that shakes the ground as he trots past. Both breeds are so beautiful, they make me want to cry, even though so different. On re-reading what I have just written, I am forced to add one more item to my list of 'tear-jerkers': the 'airs above the ground' of the Lippizaners of the Spanish Riding School in Vienna. I saw them when they came to England in the fifties, but another ambition I have is to see them perform at their home in Vienna.

By the time I was fourteen, I had collected enough stud-cards and photographs of Arabs to start a separate album for them. I took out the few I had stuck into a general scrapbook of horses, cows and hens, and replaced them in a handsome red looseleaf stamp album. Over several years I accumulated a wonderful collection but then, while I was away at school, we moved house and the album was lost. It was only when I came to Kenya and met a lady who bred Arabs and let me ride them, that I tried to find the album – alas with no success! I mourn its loss sincerely, for it was a formidable album. At the first Arab Show at Roehampton that I went to, I took a few snaps which were fairly good, and the year after some even better ones. A friend of Mummy's, Lena Ramsden, was a very knowledgeable horsey person, and through her I went to a private showing at Crabbet Park and was even introduced to Lady Wentworth, who in those days was Queen of the Arab breeders. At the Crabbet visit we had most of the stud's best animals walked past us; it was a wonderful experience. All over the place were notices that photography was forbidden, but I could not resist a furtive shot of some brood mares, which I still have.

All this brings me back to my ride on an Arab in Ceylon. I knew there were some in Colombo, because the races were divided into two sections, thoroughbreds and Arabs. Many ex-racehorses became police horses and there were some beautiful animals patrolling the streets at one stage, but later their quality and condition deteriorated when racing was banned as immoral. Several people owned horses and used to ride in the cool of the morning on the race-course. Bryan Patt (with whom I fell into the flowerbed earlier on) had a half share in a stallion, and the first time I saw him was when he was lent by Bryan to give rides at the Lipton Christmas party! It was quite a sight to see this beautiful grey stallion, with his sweeping tail, docilely walking up and down carrying tiny children. With very mixed feelings of pride, and above all pea-green with envy, I watched my son have his first ride ever and thought he could not have made a better choice. I mentioned how envious I was to Bryan and he immediately offered me a chance to have a go myself.

I hadn't ridden for about six years and after about fifteen minutes, I realised I was using some very odd muscles I never knew existed! We walked gently round the racecourse, enjoying the fresh cool of the early morning. Next time round we trotted, and then cantered. All went well until we rounded the bend and ahead was the final stretch past the grandstand. I had forgotten I was on an ex-racehorse and though he was obviously dying to go, I didn't dare let him rip for fear I couldn't stop him. We finished our ride with him pulling like a train and me hanging grimly on to the curb; next day I was almost a cripple. My arms ached and my bottom was sore. I was a wreck, but a very happy one. I wouldn't have missed it for the world!

Not long after my Paul Revere effort, the I.T.G. decided to give the customers a bit of culture and we put on *The Gioconda Smile*, which was adapted from a short story by Aldous Huxley. I was given the part of the busybody nurse and spent a lot of time wheeling poor Lew Nagel about in a bathchair. Lew was no featherweight and the wretched chair had a will of its own. Furthermore, the horrid little wheel at the back kept on running over my foot. I had a large nurse's veil to keep in place too and there were moments when I thought the front row might receive us into its laps, bathchair and all! During this show, I first met Marjorie Jayasuriya, who was a Welsh girl married to a Ceylonese. She was a first-rate actress, with a resemblance to Flora Robson and a gorgeous speaking voice. She had a long and difficult part in the play, which she carried off marvellously, and for which she received good mentions in the papers, even though the play wasn't very popular and made a loss. Poor Marjorie had one especially frightful moment one night. There was a dramatic scene with a thunderstorm raging and on a certain cue an especially fierce lightening flash would cause Marjorie, watching by the window, to exclaim, 'That was a big one!'. The cue came all right, but not the flash. Marjorie stood rooted with horror, trying to remember what line came after. A spine-chilling moment of silence followed, which to us seemed to last five minutes. Then at last came the blinding flash, and we all breathed again. It was a moot point who would get at the lights man first after the show to eat him alive . . .

Whilst rehearsals for *Gioconda* were in progress, we decided to try something entirely new for the November production. After a lot of hard work, we eventually produced seven one-act plays and ran them for six nights with two different programmes of four plays, except that one play ran all six nights. This last was a hilarious comedy, written by one of our members, about a Ceylonese family's efforts to get a rather plain daughter married off. It brought the house down every night, and we all used to stand in the wings giggling, regardless of the fact we had seen it dozens of times before. The other six plays were a mixed bag. I tried my hand at producing *The Dear Departed*, but vowed 'never again' on the first night, when my leading star forgot his lines the second he set foot on stage . . . poor Mary Calthrop, who had just had lines trouble in the play before (for some of us took two or three parts), was left shouting meaningly, 'Haven't you got anything to say, Grandpa?' I slunk away and left them to it. I couldn't just watch in cold blood. Leslie produced a small play and acted in a rather good spooky drama, so the house was full of odd people all the time, muttering lines and rehearsing madly. I think our servants thought the heat had caught up with us at last.

Instead of only selling tickets at one of the big stores in town, we did a lot of pre-selling amongst ourselves. About a dozen people each took a selection of tickets and sold them to friends, which gave a lot of publicity and saved paying the store so much commission. It also meant that the box plan opened with quite a few seats sold, which we found acted on the public psychologically. They were very inclined to wait until the show began to see what friends said, but if they saw a lot of seats sold on the plan, they would all buy too. The 'One Acts' were a rousing success, made a profit, and gave every member a chance to act, which was an advantage for one always had one or two willing types who turned up faithfully for auditions and paid their subs on the dot, but who honestly couldn't be trusted to say more than 'The carriage awaits, my lord'.

At the end of the year too, Ping came into season again, and in spite of my almost having a nervous breakdown trying to foil him, the same pi-dog again caught her. This time we didn't see it happen, but after being missing very early one morning, the wanderer suddenly reappeared and upon seeing me, dropped onto her stomach and, grinning ghastily, squirmed up to me and prostrated her wretched self at my feet. It was only too obvious what had happened, and sure enough next February she produced four pups. Again I steeled myself, and put down two, a bitch and a very ugly dog, for having seen how she lost condition in feeding three last time, I wanted to prevent the same happening again. We were due to go on leave in March, when the pups would be only just weaned, so I had to fix up homes for them and arrange for them to be picked up a week after we left. Biddy again said they would have Skip but couldn't take Ping as well, so she was to go to the Godwins when the pups had gone.

Leslie had to go on a Far East business trip on the way home, so we decided he should go ahead of me. I had a small part in a farce called *As Long as They're Happy*, so would be busy, and would leave after the last night, fly home, and wait for Leslie to join me at the Park Hill Hotel. It was horrible seeing him off and when I got home, I even got maudlin over some of his cigarette ends lying mutely in a grubby ash-tray! The days flew past, with everyone very kind about seeing I wasn't lonely and rehearsals or shows every evening. This was another of my famous cameo parts: I was a dumb blonde call-girl, and I only came in Act Two for twenty minutes. It was a lovely part, with not many lines to worry about, so I was able to enjoy the whole play. I was all done up in a very tight blue satin dress with a plunge neck, and I did a red rinse on my hair, which considerably agitated my family when I went back to England!

Just before I left Colombo, I was lying on my lonely couch one night almost asleep and with the light out, when I saw a shadowy hand come through the barred window and feel about on the dressing-table. I leapt up yelling something rude and the intruder shot off over the wall into the American Embassy next door. Our houseboy Sam, whose room was almost next door to mine, came charging gamely out waving a club, but of course it was too late by then. Only a month before, I had been typing one afternoon in the sunroom when I happened to glance out of the window and see a young Ceylonese sauntering across the lawn towards the gate carrying a small wrapped parcel in his hand. I called out 'Hi, what are you doing?' or something equally futile, to which he paid no attention, simply strolling out and riding off on a bicycle. Of course, by the time I'd got my shoes on and got out after him, he was gone. In the sitting room adjoining the sunroom, I had left my bag, which was so near that I could see it from where I was sitting if I leant over to the left. It was now open and my Parker 51, my diary and cheque-book were gone. The latter was in a black plastic wallet, and he may have thought it had money in it. I dialled 333, our 999 equivalent, and shortly after a police car arrived bursting with men, who took statements and made the place filthy with exciting little messes for fingerprints: white dust on dark surfaces, black dust on light. We all had to have our prints taken, which pleased the children no end, but it was all to no avail. Those were just a few more things to add to a vast list of valuables etc. we had pinched during our seven years in Ceylon. Most of those were taken by servants and were very hard to pin down. As soon as something was missing, they all used to accuse each other. It was horrid. One just had to make oneself lock everything up and not leave temptation in their way. Just before I left, I found that Joslin, the nanny, was stealing eggs from the nest, so I sacked her with effect from our departure, but when we came back from the U.K. she turned up and the kids loved her, so I took her back.

CHAPTER 10

Trouble on S.S. *Canberra*. Skip becomes an actress

*A*s *LONG AS THEY'RE HAPPY* came to an end, the children and I flew back to a chilly English spring and we were all welcomed back to the hurly-burly of Park Hill life. By April, 1961 I was able to inform a thunderstruck Taddy that I was having a baby in November. We were very pleased and hoped for a girl. I was very fit and have never suffered from morning sickness, so my pregnancy didn't affect our leave at all. As usual, the children caught something. This time it was chickenpox. Poor Taddy and Denis – we felt desperately sorry for them; they had had several cancellations from ill health, and there were so few guests that we didn't have to send the children away. The leave sped past and soon we were packing up once more to go. We had decided to go by sea this time. I had never been on a long sea trip, so we chose the maiden voyage of the *Canberra*. I was all agog as we climbed up the gang-plank and entered the floating luxury liner-hotel. It was all so vast and new. Some of the work wasn't even finished, we were told. We had two cabins next door to one another, beautifully furnished but with ghastly modern art on the walls which must have cost the earth, they were so obscure.

We had great fun exploring the ship, which was vast. There was a wonderful nursery for the children, a big cinema, a laundrette just down the passage from our cabins, and we each had an iron and an ironing board in the cabin. Our steward told us that many of these had been pilfered even before the ship sailed, plus bedcovers, cushions, and some of the beautiful new cellular blankets off the beds.

The second day out we started rolling a bit, and I found that I felt a lot happier if I stayed prone! Thanks to our stabilisers, it got no worse and only lasted one day, and then we put in at Naples. We didn't go ashore since Leslie had a bad sore throat and anyhow it was pouring with rain. By lunchtime, he felt so rotten, he went to see the doctor, who examined him and said he had an acute strep. throat infection

At the Park Hill Hotel. Chris and Ann.

and whisked him off to christen the hospital. There were two wards, as far as I recall; one had two old ladies in it and Leslie was installed in the other. This was all rather depressing and next day Neal was also ill with a fever and throat. The doctor came and said he must stay in bed . . . My time was spent rushing Sarah to meals and back to the nursery, visiting Leslie when I could, and looking after Neal, who was no trouble and slept a lot. Leslie had by now been joined by a large gentleman who had fallen down the stairs one night after a party. When I went to visit Leslie, he told me that the new casualty had woken up from his stupor, got out of bed without a stitch on, and wandered off to look for a nurse. When he found her she had been highly scandalised and sent him packing back to bed and decency just before I arrived! On Leslie's third day in hospital we reached Port Said, and I amused myself watching the bumboats which plied their wares beside the ship. I wondered if anyone ever cheated on the vendors by hauling up a leather pouffe and then just vanishing with it!

Just before he was due to leave his bed, Leslie had a visit from a clergyman, who kindly asked him if he would like to receive Holy Communion next morning. Poor Leslie didn't like to hurt his feelings by declining, so accepted the offer with mixed enthusiasm. I was asked to bring his dressing-gown for the occasion, and had to brief him about procedure, as it was rather a long time since he had last attended Communion. We hoped his condition had not been reported to the padre as being serious enough to warrant this bedside service!

Three days after Leslie was discharged, we reached Aden. We went ashore, feeling obscurely ashamed of being tourists, and grew very hot indeed. We were very glad to get back to the air-conditioning of the ship. You can imagine the chaos that evening when, during a film show of *The King and I*, all the lights went off, and later the air-conditioning as well. Five different times were announced as the sailing time, and finally the Chairman of the shipping line spoke over the p.a. system. He was most apologetic and said everything was being done that was possible, and he advised people to sleep on deck. In fact it was bearable in the cabin and the air-conditioning came on again at 4.00 in the morning, so we finally sailed after lunch. Just before we got to Colombo, we had the childrens' sports, in which Sarah won a race and was given a nice red ball, which caused Neal, who had refused point blank to race, to burst into tears of jealousy and recrimination. But in a later contest he was able to redeem himself and win some sweets! I wasn't really sorry when we woke up one morning to find ourselves docked in the harbour at Colombo.

We very soon settled down and plunged into rehearsals for *Arsenic and Old Lace*. Leslie had the glorious part of the mad but endearing Teddy and had to learn to play the bugle. He used to practise in the bath, and poor Skipper, who is sensitive to noises, used to run away tail between her legs, and hide till Leslie was too blue in the face to raise another puff! I was doing the décor, and in an effort to capture that ghastly Victorian cabbage-rose effect on the wallpaper, rather over-reached myself (literally, I was up on a ladder, five months pregnant, stencilling the blasted things all over the flats. Mary Calthrop was also pregnant. She acted as prompt, so there wasn't much room backstage). Altogether the effect wasn't quite as I desired. One critic said the set 'clanged like cymbals', which was a bit unkind, but the play survived it and was a great success.

Skipper came in season in July, but instead of her usual placid behaviour, she became highly attractive to Scamp, the small brown daschund next door. He fell for her in a big way and, to my horror, I found them one day on the lawn in a Very Compromising Position. I wasn't very pleased as she was eight, and I felt that was a bit old to have a family. However, we needn't have worried; nothing happened, which led us to believe she was barren.

September saw us putting on *Winslow Boy*, and I well recall sitting in the theatre watching a performance and starting to have contractions. This time I wasn't fooled, and serenely continued to have them on and off for another two months, when – a week early, bless her – Tessa was born. Having now known Tessa for seven years, I'm not at all surprised that she was a difficult birth, and only decided to appear when the specialist arrived to do a forceps delivery. I was able to respond to yet another spurious request for just 'one last push,' and that was that. We were thrilled to have a girl, apart from the fact that we were still wrangling about a suitable boy's name, whereas we had both agreed on Tessa for a daughter. I found the third child even easier; I worried far less and if she woke up and cried in the evening, I just brought her out and she lay and looked about her until I got tired of her and put her back, and off she'd go to sleep. Neal as a baby was often left to yell, out of sheer cussedness on my part. Sarah seldom cried at all; it was amazing how individual each one was.

We finished the year with a rather hurried production of *Treasure Island*, which didn't go down so well with the public and never had full houses, despite reduced prices for children and the proximity of Christmas. The cast had a great time, especially the beer drinkers at the Spy Glass Inn, who turned in impeccable performances as drunken, roystering pirates, with real beer and loud burps . . .

We saw out the Old Year as usual at home. The sound of the crackers woke Neal up and we could hear all the ships in the port hooting like mad; it was bedlam for about a quarter of an hour. Poor Skip hated it and retired under the sofa to shiver and pant, and was never able to be comforted. Pingle didn't worry and used to tear into the garden barking idiotically and adding to the din.

We had more fun and games in January, when she came in season and was frequently visited by The Hound of the Baskervilles. We named him this because we never saw more than a disappearing tail or a huge shadow vanishing over the wall, and I went insane trying to proof the garden against him. I put a barred gate over one hole in the wire fence and waited for him with one of the kids' cricket bats! One night I heard a noise from the fence and dashed out with a torch and the bat, hoping to catch him from behind. To my horror, I found a huge brown dog hanging by one hind leg caught in the wire fence. He was struggling and kicking and I don't know how he didn't dislocate his hip; his entire weight was on that one leg. I grabbed him by the base of his tail to take the weight off the leg and yelled for Leslie to bring the wire clippers. We cut him out and he vanished like smoke, not even limping. I didn't have the heart to use the bat in cold blood, and he didn't come back for a day or two! That night we heard the sound of shots and later heard that a coup to overthrow the Government had been foiled. Many top-ranking officers of the Army and Navy were involved and more than twenty were arrested. The subsequent trials dragged on literally for years, as the poor defendants either died off, committed suicide or were released suddenly. The jail was a few miles up the road from us and we used to see the procession of cars, jeeps, lorries and the armoured van, bristling with guns and troops, trailing down to the court each day. It must have cost the tax payers a small fortune.

In May Skipper became an actress. The play was another crazy farce called *Love's a Luxury*, and Skip was chosen to take the part of 'Rollie', a lap dog belonging to the leading lady. She turned in a polished performance and even got a mention by one reviewer as 'taking his bow like a seasoned trouper,' so even the critic thought she was a he! I used to watch her most nights. The only mistake she made was when she turned her back to the audience once. She has been moulting rather badly, as she does sometimes, and her normally decent rear end, lacking its usual ample bustles, was far from being her best view! It wasn't the night the critic was there or he would never have called her 'him'!

About this time the Group was having a spot of adultery in its midst and there was a lot of gossip flying about. It was all very sad really, and I got involved with one of the wronged wives, who came and cried and asked my help. There were five children involved in the two families, and it was some months before it was all sorted out and everyone returned to their original partners. One doesn't realise how frightful these upheavals are until one meets the people involved and gets dragged in to help. Somehow, out East it seems to happen so often. Couples swop all the time and everyone has a wonderful time gossiping over the coffee cups or Mah-Jong tiles (but not over the bridge table, I think, it doesn't strike me as *that* sort of a game at all, but then I don't play!).

I decided that as Ping had kept out of trouble for a year, we might try to find a nice husband for her. I badly wanted her to have some fluffy pups, so finally asked a friend who had a small black poodle. She assured me Pookie would be most pleased to oblige, so I sent the children to play round at Anne's for the morning and prepared to welcome the bridegroom. He arrived by car all merry and bright and his owner departed hastily, saying she'd call back for him later. There followed a farce rather similar to the time when I tried to marry off Skipper in Calcutta. Alas, poor Pookie, all his enthusiasm came to nought, despite my assistance with cushions and a helping hand. He was just not tall enough to cope. Poor Pingle got sick of the whole business and walked away disgusted, leaving a breathless Pookie and me sitting on the grass looking rather silly! It was a moot point who was the most frustrated . . . After that, I tried another friend, who had a much bigger shaggy dog called Bosco. We had a most successful session. Bosco arrived, did what had to be done, and after ten minutes was wandering round the garden exploring! Everything happened so quickly that I wondered whether there would be any pups, but nine weeks later they arrived on the dot – three of them. It was impossible to tell which was going to be long haired, but after a few weeks, one was short, one wiry and one long. I was very pleased this time that two went to good friends of mine and that I was able to keep track of them. Ginny Godwin had the bitch, a nice bright brown, short-haired, and the image of her mother. Marjorie Jayasuriya had the shaggy one and called him 'Mr Hoskins' after a character in *Arsenic and Old Lace*. She also had two cats named Abbey and Martha after the old ladies in the play. The third pup went to a friend of a friend, who left Colombo soon after, and I never knew what happened to the puppy.

CHAPTER 11

Much travelling and lots of disasters. My radio career begins

ARLY IN 1963 we had the good fortune to pay another visit to a National Park, and this time we were able to take the children with us. The Perkins had originally intended this trip, but then for some reason had to alter their arrangements, so generously offered the booking to us, for the Park resthouses were booked up months in advance. We spent a very happy long weekend at Wilpattu, which was a wooden bungalow on stilts. You drove the car underneath to park and climbed upstairs to the house, which had a veranda running all round it, and so up to the rough bedrooms, with partitioned walls and a thatched roof. We did, however, have a proper push-and-pull loo, and we discovered a charming treefrog who lived under the watertank there. You got used to two beady eyes watching! The night-time was wonderful. We used to sit on the veranda with our oil lamps hissing, listening to the jungle noises. A herd of buffalo came through in the night and made a tremendous noise – most exciting. Next morning we went out early with the tracker and saw a leopard bounding away across the grass and also found a bear very close to us. Ceylon bears are small, about four feet long, and short-legged, with a very tatty, degenerate air about them. They also have huge black whiffly noses, and their muzzles are a dirty white. The one we saw looked very grubby; he had obviously been at an anthill and his nose was covered in mud. He was scratching his bottom in a rather unlovely fashion against a tree, but we stopped and watched him, thrilled to bits, until he shambled off about his business. We also saw crocodiles, buffalo, sambhur and dozens of lovely birds. We left on the third day with great reluctance to return to the urban life once more.

April found us ready for our home leave, and this time we decided to try and rent a house rather than stay at the hotel again. We were very lucky to find an adorable house at Hadlow, near Tonbridge, and had a most happy three months there. The house was quite old and was off the main road in a cul-de-sac. Next door was the pub, which suited Leslie, and a bit further up was the church. The furniture was of the clean but worn variety, and we hired a television and had some cosy evenings viewing. I tend to be a bit of an addict, especially where wrestling is concerned, and Saturday afternoon is always held sacred!

While we were away, Skipper was cared for by our friends the Collins, and Ping by the Godwins. It wasn't until after we returned to Colombo that Sheila Collins told me the ghastly time they had the day Skipper vanished . . . Sheila had been busy packing some big tin trunks when a friend had called with a dog in the car. Skipper must have followed the car out when it left and the gate was shut on her. Some hours later her absence was noticed and a great search began. Poor Sheila was nearly frantic, and got to the lunatic phase of even opening up the tin trunks in case Skip was doing a mistletoe bough act inside! They rang the police, sent out search parties, and altogether had a very worrying time until next day, when the police rang Barry asking him to come and see a dog they had 'in custody'. A small, dishevelled Skipper, with a piece of string round her neck, greeted Barry with such enthusiasm that it left the police in no doubt that she knew where she belonged. I believe she had been found in some small shop in the back streets of a type known as a 'boutique'. This always tickled us, for we knew how very different its Parisian namesake would be, with perhaps one beautiful expensive hat tastefully arranged with a string of pearls in the window. Colombo boutiques were usually of mud and palm thatch, selling a small selection of groceries and sometimes tea, served in tiny handmade earthenware cups called 'chatties', which were usually thrown away after being used, so cheap were they.

The Collins told us about this when we came back off leave and I felt very sorry they had been put to such trouble and anxiety; it is the penalty one pays when one looks after other people's pets, but mercifully doesn't seem to happen too often.

We had a disastrous return, in fact. It started on the ship, the *Cathay*, when a seven-year-old girl fell down the staircase well from 'A' Deck to 'D' Deck . . . Neal came running into the cabin one afternoon looking very white and said someone had fallen down the stairs. I went out, expecting to see someone who had slipped down a few steps, perhaps, and was shocked to see a great crowd and the child lying unconscious on the floor outside the dining room. Luckily we were near Malta, so we changed course and put off the child and her family at Valetta. About a week later we heard that she had been discharged from hospital and had only had a fractured humerus and slight head injuries! I used to look at that drop and shudder; it was about thirty feet, and next day netting was put along the banisters along the staircase. Everyone was very subdued for a day or two and one noticed far fewer noisy children running wild about the ship. There were too many complacent parents who used to say, 'I don't know where Johnny goes all day; I only see him at mealtimes.'

When we finally docked in Colombo, we were in pretty poor shape. Neal had a temperature of 102 and looked pale and listless, Tessa had been coughing a lot and I was just at the fruitiest stage of a frightful cold, streaming and trumpeting incessantly and wishing death would come soon. We were met by Ginny Godwin, who said that we had not yet had our furniture moved from the old house in Horton Terrace to the new one in Gower St. We all trailed back to the old house, which looked gloomy and depressing with all the stuff packed ready for the move. It was only the great kindness of Joan Street next door, who invited us all to lunch, that saved our sanity. The Streets were a charming Australian family with five children, so it was really marvellous of Joan to take us on, germs and all. She lent me Kleenex, put Neal to lie down, fed those of us who could eat and throughout this ordeal managed to give the impression that she actually enjoyed it! We decided that rather than stay on in the old house, Leslie should go to the office and get a lorry so that we could move everything that afternoon. I put Tessa to sleep in the bedroom, bare as it was, with the air-conditioner on, and spent the afternoon drearily waiting for the lorry to arrive. I was on my own as Neal and Sarah went with Leslie. Finally the lorry arrived, Tessa woke up in an abominable black mood, and I felt nearer and nearer to death, with a raging sore throat now to add to my troubles. We did manage the move by nightfall, leaving only some tea-chests of stuff which we'd brought with us on the ship.

If I had thought that was a bad day, the next one eclipsed it in ghastliness. I tottered about unpacking as best I could, and Leslie went off to Horton Terrace to collect the tea-chests. I flopped out on the bed and was just dropping off when Leslie returned, to inform me, as tactfully as he could, that the Horton Terrace house had been burgled in the night, the air-conditioner taken out of the wall, and the one tea-chest that Customs had opened had been emptied. We then had the task of getting the police and finding out what was missing. The tea-chests had their contents listed so we knew we'd lost some nice curry dishes, a new thermos flask Leslie had bought in Aden, a new Triang engine of Tessa's, and a super Phoenix dish with lights under it that I had been given by a grateful Companion Book Club for introducing a new member. This was bad enough, but then we remembered with horror that there had been a cardboard box we had filled at the last moment with odds and ends, not listed. Bit by bit, we'd recall things, like the new two-way baby alarm, lampshades, and a lot of things you couldn't get in Ceylon such as mustard, elastic that really worked, nail varnish and hair lacquer. The final straw to that hellish day came in the evening, when I suddenly remembered a plastic bag with all my costume jewellery in it, which then reminded me of a small box containing my pearls. Mummy and Daddy had given them to me as a wedding present and I had worn them at our wedding. Snatching up a box of Kleenex, I bolted to the bathroom and there Leslie found me some minutes later howling my eyes out. He has the most sympathetic shoulder I know for crying on to, and after a bit I recovered enough to emerge in time to greet the Collins, who had come to bring us Skipper and see how we were getting on ... We sat on the veranda and told them the long, sad saga and felt a bit better afterwards. We never did get anything back. I sometimes wonder who is wearing my pearls and what the thieves made of the baby alarm, as it was a new gadget in those days.

As occasionally happens to families, we continued with our bad luck. Five days after we got back I was almost voiceless, Tessa got measles and Leslie went down with 'flu ... The only bright spot was that I found my plastic bag with the costume jewellery in it, stuffed away at the back of a drawer. I can only presume that I had been in such a daze that I'd honestly never recalled seeing it, let alone unpacking it, which I must have done. I felt an awful idiot having to go to the police station and tell them to strike it off the list. Soon Tessa was on the mend, so it looked as if we might be out of the wood, but no. One day when Joslin was off, Neal fell and gashed his hand and shoulder on some wire. One cut was deep and bled a lot, so I rang the Streets to ask if I could leave the girls with them while I took Neal to the doctor. As usual, they rose magnificently to the occasion and I took a tearful Neal off to the doctor. No stitches were necessary, but a tetanus jab was given amid heartrending yells. As if this were not enough, that evening I noticed that Sarah was passing blood and had a temperature of 103° . . . The doctor, not our usual nice one, who was on leave, turned out rather reluctantly and gave us a penicillin prescription. He also gave us instructions for a urine test and also a blood test next day. In the evening Sarah's temperature soared again to nearly 104° and I rang the doctor. He didn't offer to come but said we were to give her Febrilix. Leslie drove out for some, and it turned out to be marvellous. In half an hour her temperature was down to 102°, and in three hours it was normal. Next day the doctor called in a specialist, who gave her a very thorough examination and said she should be in hospital except that she was obviously getting measles, which would not be welcome. She had nephritis, he said, a kidney infection. The spots appeared that day and after that she was much better. The urine slowly cleared and she was quite bright. Unfortunately my diary stops at this point for several months, so I assume all was well, but when I was writing all this, I remember being amazed that so many awful things should happen to us in just four weeks. Normally, we are a pretty healthy family, so I suppose we are caught on the hop when things do go wrong; up to this time I'd had a theory, borne out by observing other people, that the more one worried, the more troubles would come to one, but now I'm not so sure. I know I got to the stage of dreading meeting friends with the casual query on their lips, 'How are you?', because invariably I had a tale of fresh disaster to tell.

The rest of the year passed peacefully enough, with some one-act plays to keep us occupied in October. Not long after that, I met Vernon Abeysekere at an I.T.G. party. Taking a chance, I asked him if the film reviewers on his programme needed any qualifications. Vernon had a weekly programme on Radio Ceylon called 'The Arts This Week', in which books, plays, films and concerts were reviewed and discussed. We always had a wireless in the dressing-room on Friday night after a play was on to hear what the reviewer had to say about us. To my great delight, Vernon asked if I'd like to do a film review next week, and that was the start of my small but enjoyable career in broadcasting.

I found out that, as I had anticipated, it was a very pleasant chore
being a film critic! I was given a cinema pass to admit two free, to
whichever film I had chosen, and each Thursday, when the new films
came out, I would sally forth. The first time I waved my pass at the
box office I was slightly dashed to find that no one went for the
manager to usher me reverently to my seat, but nevertheless I felt very
important as I settled there with my notebook and pencil. Next day I
had to see the second film, and as the broadcast was at eight in the
evening, I had to go to the 3.30 showing. Then I would fly home,
bash out the review, polish it up, and be ready to leave at 7.30. I really
enjoyed our programme. I used to sit in the little studio watching for
the red light and wondering if anything was going to go wrong.
Vernon seemed pretty lighthearted about it. You would be told how
long your bit would have to last, which entailed a lot of work at home
reading the script aloud with a watch beside you, hoping that nerves
wouldn't make you gabble it, thus causing a 'short fall' at the end of
the programme. Usually we finished with about a minute or two in
hand, but on one occasion there was a ten-minute 'shortfall'. This was
later on in my career, when Radio Ceylon, which was very
Government-controlled, started censoring things. One young chap
had come to review a book by James Baldwin and when he was
saying a few words for the engineers to 'balance', he happened to read
the opening part of his script, which had something frightful in it. I
think it was some bad word like 'adultery' or 'prostitution' and the
lady in the control room popped out like a petrified rabbit and asked
to read the script. Up till then we had been uncensored but she sat
down in the control room then and there, and we had to go on air
with the poor man not knowing if he was going on or not. After a
few minutes she peered through the glass and made suitably reluctant
washing-out motions of her hands and shook her head, so the book
review was cut out. I gathered afterwards it wasn't just the language;
there were fears of upsetting Americans with some of Baldwin's
opinions. After that we were told that scripts would all have to be read
by Authority the day before transmission, which in my case was an
awful nuisance, I had to go to a 3.30 film, rush home, write it up, go
to the 6.30 film after that, write it up, deliver the script next day and
hope it would be passed. It always was, but I sometimes couldn't resist
pulling the lady producer's leg. 'I've done a good one today,' I'd say to

her, 'I've said the leading lady was about as animated as Mrs Bandaranaike at a political rally.' I think it really worried her that I *might* say something, poor thing. Perhaps I ought to explain that after her husband was assassinated, Mrs Bandaranaike went into politics and, as the weeping widow, got herself made Prime Minister. Her best friend couldn't say she was a ball of fire, with her sad heavy face and her monotonous voice. She hadn't even been elected an M.P. for any constituency, though she said it wasn't necessary; she *knew* everyone would vote for her anyhow... I could ramble on for a long time about Ceylon's politicians, and I have some hilarious cuttings in my scrap-book, which make startling reading coming from those who ran the poor little country. But I'd better not – I may want to go back there one day.

Apart from film reviews, I also did a short, witty (I hoped) talk on a woman's programme about how to please a new husband, and both Leslie and I did a sort of Desert Island discs, choosing records and talking about them. Our best broadcasts, I think, were towards the end of that tour, when we did a kind of 'Twenty Questions' in a series of about six recorded shows. I was in the team and Leslie was the scorer. We had a lot of fun and I felt quite Jack Train-ish on a good night when I guessed right several times. We used to have a mystery visitor and we would all blindfold ourselves and try to guess who it was. One time they fooled us and chose Leslie, and it took me far longer than it should have to guess who it was. I got told off very soon after the programme started for saying 'My God!' in a loud voice, so I had to watch my language. It was a bit of an effort, and sometimes something would slip out and I'd give an agonised look at the control room, but although it was a taped programme, they would only stop to re-record if someone fell down dead, so my profane language went out to Ceylon listeners regardless. I was very sorry to leave my broadcasting career behind me when we left Ceylon. I remember my last film review was *West-Side Story*, which I took Leslie to see and we thought it was first-class. I expect sometimes listeners thought I was a real crank in what I said about the films. One frightful Italian (dubbed) epic I had been forced to see for lack of any better fare had a perfectly horrible battle scene in it. I am always on the lookout to see how animals in films are treated, especially horses, who seem to me to have a beastly time, being shot at, thrown to the ground, galloped to death and jumped over precipices. I don't care how much the producer says they like it, are trained for it and never get hurt. Anyone who knows horses can tell when they are scared. In this film I noticed something odd about the attacking enemy, who were falling into concealed pits covered in grass and bushes. Then I realised that the wretched animals were blindfolded and being ridden into pits and over river-banks into the water. It ruined the film for me. I felt like crying, and knowing how long it takes to film a two-minute sequence, I expect the poor things suffered for days. In the same way, *The Misfits* was ruined for me by the brutal way in which the mares were thrown, tied up and left in the blazing sun, with small bewildered foals nuzzling their mothers as they lay helpless. There was also a long and horrible battle between Clark Gable and a wild stallion. At times the beast was a dripping, panting mass of flesh with the rope tight about its neck. I read later that Gable had insisted in doing this scene himself and his wife reckoned it killed him; I'm afraid I muttered, 'Serve him right.' He's not my type, anyway.

Another nice film that had a nasty bit in it for anyone with good eyesight was *The Swiss Family Robinson*. There was a hilarious race between the family Robinson and their animals, but how many people noticed that the ostrich someone was riding was blindfolded with a mask over its head painted to look like an ostrich? How many thought that the tiny monkey *tied* to the back of the Great Dane was simply gibbering with fear as it was bounced interminably along? This is another of my hobby horses, and when I mentioned the blindfolded horses in my review, I don't expect anyone else had noticed or even cared. For this reason I never went to see *Lawrence of Arabia* or *Ben Hur*, and have steered clear of 'epics' ever since. I feel that if someone is spending millions on a film, he won't worry if a few horses are written off.

Once again, I have wandered off the subject and poor Skipper hasn't been mentioned at all in this chapter, though she and Ping were around all right, sitting on our feet, begging for food, barking at intruders and helping bring up the kids. Actually, it was early in 1964 that Skipper was almost killed – by a fridge, of all things. In late January Leslie's mother came out to stay for a few weeks. We were deeply involved in *Witness for the Prosecution*, Agatha Christie's brilliant 'whodunit', and just before she went back to England, she came to our first night and saw me in my immortal cameo portrayal as Greta, the typist with adenoids, and Leslie as Mr Myers Q.C. She was most impressed with our efforts. I think she'd been expecting something in the style of 'Much Binding Ladies' Guild of Drama' in the Village Hall, (proceeds in aid of a new roof for the Vicarage). In fact we all felt it was one of our best shows, and later in Nairobi, when we went to see a professional production of the same show, we found many faults that we as amateurs would never have allowed and were horrified to find much of it was played for cheap laughs. Anyhow, all this is leading up to the fact that Mother departed by plane, her first flight ever, just before the last night of the play. We came home that night and I went into the kitchen to get myself a glass of milk. Skipper followed me in and was sniffing about by the fridge, which was frequently the refuge of rats. I was at the sink when I heard an odd sort of grunt and turned to see Skip lying on the floor twitching. Guessing she had been electrocuted, I switched off the fridge and picked her up. She looked awful. She had lost control of her bladder and was soaked, and had bitten her tongue, which was bleeding. (She still has the scar too.) She was shivering and scared and I walked her about and soothed her, and when she seemed calmer, we went to bed and she had a good night. Next day she was very shivery and I took her to the vet, who, to my surprise, recommended rubbing the pads of her feet with a ruler. I can't recall exactly what this was meant to do – something about earthing her perhaps. Anyhow, feeling a bit silly, I did it, and she's still with us, five years later. The electrician who looked at the fridge said there was a bad fault in it, so perhaps we were lucky it wasn't one of us who caught a few volts.

For the rest of 1964 I can recall very little, and if I kept a diary that year, I seem to have lost it. I know we did *Pool's Paradise* in July and Leslie was a parson again. It was written by the same author as *See How They Run*, and it was just as nutty and as well-received.

1965 was ushered in with a strike of all the Swimming Club staff on New Year's Eve. They were dissatisfied with the Christmas bonus so they all sat glumly outside the gates while inside enthusiastic volunteers manned the bar, ran the catering and generally ensured that despite efforts to the contrary, it was the best New Year's party ever! For a month the club was run by a volunteer staff of members and it was fun selling ices, which was my contribution. In the end the staff all returned to work at a considerable saving to the club, who had saved a month's wages and done a roaring bar trade.

In February Sarah was taken to an e.n.t. specialist after a lot of sore throats. Previously he had been reluctant to take out her tonsils, but this time I casually mentioned the nephritis and he immediately said the tonsils and adenoids must come out. Apparently there was a risk that the infection could reach the kidneys via the tonsils, which seemed odd to me. Anyhow, in she went, and we were very lucky that the Frazer Nursing home is enlightened enough to allow mothers to stay and sleep with the children. I had a bed next to hers and was able to be with her until she was carried down, half doped, to the theatre. She was given penicillin jabs twice a day at first to stop any infection and they were painful, poor kid. I gave her ten cents a time for them, which helped, and after the first day, when she was a bit weepy, she recovered fast. We were out in three days. I feel very strongly that it is positively cruel to maroon a small scared child in hospital feeling ill and lonely, among strange faces and unless the mother is a complete ass (which regrettably, some are) she ought to be allowed to stay all the time. Anyhow, when Neal's turn came a few months later, I knew the ropes and we spent a comparatively pleasant three days again in the Frazer. The worst part is certainly waiting for them to be brought back, limp and blood stained, with that fearsome tube in the mouth to aid breathing. I couldn't help thinking how different it all was to my own t. and a. removal at the London Clinic, and how I had my 17th birthday there and fell in love with the anaesthetist, giving him a huge slice of cake. It didn't hold him, though, and I never saw him again . . .

April came and with it news of a big change in our lives.

CHAPTER 12

1965. Farewell Colombo.
Hello, Ireland, Jambo, Nairobi!

IT WAS JUST AS WELL that we had something different to think about at this time; in terms of health, we were just getting over our second Bad Patch. Leslie had had a mysterious high fever for several days at a time when he was supposed to be rehearsing for *Doctor's Dilemma*. The wretched play had a jinx on it from the start, and it was a wonder that the poor producer wasn't a nervous wreck. No sooner was a part cast than someone else would drop out. When it was finally cast and rehearsals were under way, there was a muddle over the theatre booking and we almost cancelled the whole show. Then there was doubt about Leslie's being fit in time, but in the end our problems were solved by a new and slightly later booking of the theatre, which allowed some more much-needed time. I was very busy helping with costumes, which was a most rewarding job. On the night they looked really superb, and the cost of them was very reasonable. I also had a small part at the beginning as a maid, which I enjoyed. We had a nasty moment on about the third night of the show when a young Ceylonese chap, who had the part of a waiter in the first act, never showed up until the play had begun. It was possible to cut his bit, right at the end, when only Leslie and he were on stage, and this we had to do, much to Leslie's surprise when the curtain closed suddenly on him. About ten minutes before he was due on stage, the errant waiter had turned up in a taxi and tumbled out in evening dress, extremely drunk and with a weeping girl trying to delay him. He tottered into the dressing room and expressed his intention of going on as usual. I hurriedly summoned the stage manager and his helper, both brawny rugger hearties, and they very rapidly dissuaded the waiter, who slunk off. He didn't appear the next night either; apparently he didn't dare, but did have the decency to write a grovelling letter to the producer.

On top of all these upsets, we had Tessa ill with a form of bronchitis.

At the beginning she ran a temperature of nearly 105°, and that night had convulsions . . . I have a vivid and terrible memory of bending over the cot at 3 a.m., watching in horror as she champed her teeth and waved her arms about, then fell perfectly quiet with her eyes slightly crossed. I honestly thought she had gone mental and flew in to Leslie, who sleepily peered at her and said she looked all right to him. I rushed to dear Dr Spock, as by this time I had realised it must be convulsions, and he was his usual reassuring self as I leafed though the pages of his wonderful book. What a comfort he is! By this time, Tessa was asleep and when she had another milder fit two hours later, I wasn't half so worried. I called the doctor that morning and he brought a specialist. She had X-rays and physiotherapy, and in the end lost the frightful cough she had had for so many weeks. It had become so bad that we used to take her out for a walk before breakfast to try and take her mind off it.

Early morning and that 'first cough of the day' was always the worst. All the children had an odd bout of sickness, starting with the girls meeting with monotonous regularity in the bathroom one night. Tessa went everywhere in the house accompanied by her 'sick bucket', which mildly amused us, but the fun wore thin after the first day. Neal, mercifully, was only sick once and after that we were out of the wood.

I was having coffee with Margaret Southwell one morning in April, 1965 and she seemed most eager for me to ring Leslie, who had rung earlier before I arrived. She kept asking me whether I hadn't better ring him, so at last I did.

You've always wanted to see Kilimanjaro,' he said triumphantly, 'Well, now you will. We've been posted to Kenya. We go to Nairobi after our leave in November!'

I didn't know what to do, I was so excited. All my life I had longed to go to Africa and see the wild animals there. I never missed a film about that continent: for instance *Where No Vultures Fly*, *Simba*, *King Solomon's Mines*, *Something of Value* – you name it, I'd seen it. However, it was one of my pipe dreams; I never even knew Lipton's had an office in Kenya.

The next two months were the hectic, emotional mixture one goes through when one leaves a lovely home and good friends to go to a new and also lovely place. There was so much to be done, stuff to be sold and sorted, trunks to be packed, permits and papers to be arranged, our last play to be done. This was the ideal one for us to bow out with. It was *Breath of Spring*, and for a change, I had the bigger part as the dithery old lady who tries to be a successful fur thief. Leslie was the detective who almost caught us and I must say it was a hilarious show, with full houses almost every day. It was also amazing how many furs we managed to collect as props, considering the warm Colombo climate!

As the time grew nearer for our departure in July, we plunged into selling up an accumulation of possessions, ranging from old pictures to china and movie film equipment. I put an advertisement in the paper and we had a very lively time coping with the flood of buyers who turned up. It was fascinating trying to guess what each person was interested in buying, and several times some ancient gentleman, clad in grubby old clothes, would reluctantly inch out his wallet from some inner recess to reveal that it was stuffed with hundred rupee notes. Often the bargaining was fast and furious and if one's opponent had a sense of humour, it could be a lot of fun. One evening quite late three young Ceylonese turned up, having heard through a relative that we were in business. They roamed about the house peering at what remained of our possessions and trying to persuade us to part with them. It was all very light-hearted, and in the end I sold several knick-knacks I hadn't intended parting with, including a china wall-clock made in Holland, which had been given us by a shipping line (awkward to pack). Another such item was a brass bell won by me in the Sack Race on board the *Cathay*. The highlight of our Great Bargain Sale came when we had a lively auction for the electric car racing set (always a bone of contention in the family; it took hours to set up, and two cars only between three children was death to a peaceful race). One would-be buyer was miles away up country, one was with us listening as Leslie relayed to him the phone's latest bid. In the end, the up-country buyer got it for about double what we had paid for it originally. I had one devastatingly handsome gentleman, who came several times with a pretty wife in a sari. He bought a lot of our china. I liked the idea of his having it, but I didn't feel that way about another buyer, rather plump and very prosperous, who stirred our offerings with a disdainful finger, telling me all about his own cameras, electric shavers, projectors, hair dryers and coffee percolators, all of which were bigger and better than ours. He then made some very small bids and I was thankful that in the end he went away with very little.

As the days flashed past, we became more and more conscious of the wrench it would be. We made arrangements for the servants to be taken on by the Mitchells, who were to take our place. They had been in Nairobi so it was a straight swap. The dogs, after obtaining the right certificates, were booked to sail a few days before we left. Stan and Margaret Holland would be in Nairobi to look after them, as the Mitchells were also going on leave at the same time as ourselves.

A few days before we left, we threw a Chinese chow lunch party. We had a Chinese restaurant quite nearby, and it made a change from curry. On the day of the party a Ceylonese friend, with whom we had acted in one or two plays, sent us a superb silver salver. It was such a generous gesture; we were most touched. More was to follow. The Tea Department of Lipton's summoned us one afternoon for a drink, and we were given a silver tray engraved with our names and the date, and were formally presented with the two oil paintings of Ceylon scenes that we had chosen earlier. Another friend, who had been in *Doctors' Dilemma* with us, popped round one day and diffidently handed me a wonderful mille feuille cake, saying rather shyly that his aunt had made it and it was probably ghastly – just a little something . . . Finally the International Theatre Group gave us a party and presented me with a beautiful silver and tortoiseshell pendant and Leslie with an engraved silver beer-mug. It was all too much. I felt like crying and I am never any good at goodbyes. The I.T.G. had given us so much pleasure; we were happy and proud to have been members, and even now, almost four years since we left Colombo, we have not yet taken up acting again. We keep saying we must, but sometimes feel that it could never be the same, but if we do go to an amateur show sometimes, I have the most awful pangs of envy that I'm not in on all the back-stage dramas and general goings-on. It's not enough to be just 'audience'; one wants to be part of it again, so I expect soon we shall take it up.

A goodbye that was just as bad was seeing the dogs off on the *Springbank*. We took them up to the First Officer's cabin, met the Captain, and were told that they were in good hands, that the cadets usually looked after dogs on the ship and they would live as family. I was dying to launch into a welter of advice about their care, but even I could see that the officers might not be that interested in hearing about Skipper's gremlins, or how she often tries to bury her dinner with her nose, heaping invisible earth on to it. I couldn't tell them that if this was done on a polished floor, her damp nose made a fascinating noise, like a frightened mouse. Nor could I tell them how Ping is shy of strangers and prefers a hand to sniff before getting a hearty pat. Anyhow, we left them tied to the washbasin in the First Officer's cabin, Skip with her head on one side, Ping with her ears pricked, both unable to believe we were *leaving* them. They both raised their voices in despair, and we hurried away feeling traitors, to an empty home with no welcome when we unlocked the door.

Finally came the worst goodbye of the lot. The car had come for us, the luggage was in the boot, Leslie had done a last check that we had left nothing. Tall John, the cook, with hairy ears and face, fat old Joslin and kind, cheerful Joseph, the houseboy, were all lined up on the veranda to say goodbye. I had dreaded this moment, knowing how emotional the Ceylonese can be. I had expected Joslin to be the most tearful; she had seen all the children grow up for seven years and indeed her eyes were full of tears as we shook hands. But it was poor Joseph who shocked me. He had always been such a happy, smiling chap, willing to do anything from climbing a coconut tree to fetching the guinea pigs in if it rained. Somehow, I hadn't expected him to be so affected, but there he stood, tears pouring down his face. I have a lump in my throat as I write this; it made me feel awful. Choked with tears myself, I hurriedly shook his hand and shot into the car. As we settled in, Neal said with awful clarity, 'Why is Joseph crying?' Poor child, both Leslie and I snarled at him to keep quiet with frightful venom and drove off hurriedly, swallowing hard.

This leave Ann had managed to find us a small semi-detached house on the main Tonbridge-Sevenoaks road, in her village of Hilden-borough. It was only ten minutes drive from her own house, which was very convenient, and her two, Geoff and Amanda, now 12 and 10 respectively, were able to come and go on their cycles. Our three were rather envious, but Ann lent them two old scooters, and they got a lot of pleasure out of those. The children soon got to know some of their neighbours and were a good source of local news. We were only just down the road from the church and one day they came rushing in with the news that there was to be a funeral. They had spent a long time breathing down the grave-digger's neck, as far as I could gather, and were full of hope that they might be allowed to gatecrash the interment that afternoon. I vetoed this hurriedly but said they could watch the hearse from a distance from *outside* the churchyard. I wasn't sure how much to encourage this morbid interest, but I could remember my own youthful interest in coffins and wreaths and death in general, and they reported later that there were lots of lovely flowers and people in black.

Tessa, as usual, became a centre of attraction – or should it be notoriety? It was early on in that leave when she came to me one day complaining of her head hurting. Thinking she had bumped it, I gave her an absent-minded pat and glanced casually at her head. To my horror, I saw distinct signs of life and closer inspection showed that our exports from Ceylon had not stopped short at paintings and silverware. She was simply alive with head lice . . .

I couldn't wait to tell Ann the good news. I rang her immediately! We got rather silly about it all, but I persuaded her to drive forth at once in search of something suitable for the case.

We waited for her arrival whilst I delivered a lecture on Parasites, their Life and Ways, to a fascinated audience and then sat the patient down over some newspaper and cut off most of her hair. It wasn't a bad effort and she was rather pleased, prinking about in front of the mirror and deciding to change her name to Peter. Then Ann arrived, having had a rather prolonged search to find a chemist that was open on early closing day. She handed me a parcel; 'I made it *quite* clear it wasn't for me,' she said severely as we unwrapped a bottle of white liquid, courtesy of Jeyes, and a vicious looking fine tooth comb took me back to school days when we had been 'Overrun' and had had to submit to tooth-combing daily for weeks – very painful.

We then doused Tessa's hair liberally with the stuff and combed out the corpses, but for weeks the nits remained clinging to the hair. Inevitably we discussed how such a thing could happen in *our family*. We decided that school must be to blame, in spite of the fact that it was affiliated to Cheltenham Ladies College . . . The amazing thing was that Sarah had never had any, even though she had been sharing a double bed with Tessa for the previous week. We only told a select few about the reason for our daughters crew-cut, but I did overhear her telling our daily all about 'little eggs in my hair'. I waited breathlessly for her to give notice but she never did. When we left, I hid the bottle right at the top of the hot cupboard. I often wonder if anyone ever found it. As the house was often let to people from abroad, I expect it may actually have been used . . .

One of the highlights of this leave was a caravan trip across Ireland. Neal was now eight and was to start at Dulwich College Prep. School in September. We felt he should have a nice holiday first, so in August we sailed across the Irish Sea in British Railways' brand-new and exorbitantly expensive ferry, with the car we had hired that leave, a large white Zephyr. We picked up a handsome caravan at a large site outside Dublin and spent that first night on the site. At midnight we were plunged into total darkness as the place had its own generator and they weren't prepared to waste it. Almost at once the children woke up, bewailing their fate:

'Mummy, I can't see.'

'Turn on a light, Mummy, I don't like it.'

'Mummy, the light's gone out.'

I had to explain why, and I suppose we did without, but next day we bought night-lights. The children have always had some sort of light for excursions to the bathroom.

We had a pleasant trip for a week, though the weather was not too good, and we met a lot of charming but neglected donkeys, which the children wanted to adopt. We had a lot of trouble over a dog who came to us one evening after we had settled in a layby. He looked very like Pingle and had obviously been in the wars, with a cut face and a scar on his lame hind leg. Sarah immediately adopted him and I fed him with fried bread in vast quantities, which he wolfed down. We had a look round and found a farm nearby, with a small donkey and cart tied up by the front door. We knocked and asked the farmer who came whether he'd mislaid a dog. He had and called it half-heartedly, saying it strayed a lot and had recently been run over by a car. We left the dog with him and departed, with me wondering if the poor donkey was to be left harnessed to the cart all night; by that time it was getting dark.

The dog came back a few minutes later and a demand that he be allowed into the van was cruelly vetoed by Father. It began to rain and we renewed our pleas on his behalf.

'Let him go home, he'll only make the van dirty,' was the sensible parent's answer, so he stayed all night, huddled under the hedge, sustained by more fried bread smuggled out to him by me. In the morning he was joined early by Sarah in her anorak, and we have pictures of them huddled together in the rain under the hedge. We left him with great regret. He was obviously starved of affection, poor beast. Although they may be horsey people, the Irish are not renowned for their care of animals and certainly we never saw any horse or donkey that looked really well cared-for. It rather surprised us, therefore, when we returned to Dublin for a couple of days, to find it had an excellent zoo. We were so taken with it, we visited it twice in two days. It was not a very large zoo, but much of it consisted of open-air paddocks, and the centre-piece was an extensive lake, around which were a large selection of wild-fowl, presumably pinioned. There were roomy aviaries which one could walk through, and mercifully few of the horrid Victorian-type of cages made of cement and thick bars. I have not been to a zoo since we came to East Africa, and I confess that I am not keen; to my way of thinking, once you have seen any animal in its wild state, it is never the same again behind bars, especially if it is a lion or cheetah. As for circuses, nothing would induce me ever to set foot in one again if it had any big cats or bears; I feel strongly that dogs and horses and chimps enjoy showing off, but if expressions are anything to go by, big cats loathe the humiliation of leaping through hoops and sitting on pedestals. Why do we wish to see such horrors as elephants doing handstands, lions walking a tightrope, or bears riding bicycles?

I see I'm off on yet another of my hobby-horses, but I must just tell of the crowning insult. A certain circus came to Kenya from India, complete with elephants, tigers and lions, and where did they put up their beastly Big Top? Within a mile of Nairobi National Park! I wondered if the lion tamer ever bothered to pay the Park a visit to see what a lion can really look like, but I decided he didn't bother (not interested? scared?) – otherwise he would never have been able to put on his wretched act again. I often wonder why the Government here let the circus in, but hundreds of people went, and, I expect, loved it. None of our family did, and I knew that if I saw the cages, I would lose a lot of sleep. Of necessity, a travelling circus cannot allow large cages for its prisoners.

We can now go back to Ireland. Looking back on that trip, I think one of the nicest memories was of a lunch we had in Galway. We had Chinese chow, of all things, and it was even served by a Chinese waiter, or he might have been Vietnamese, Burmese or Japanese. Anyhow, he looked right. I quote from my diary:

'Kids had 5/- lunch, orange-juice, pork chop, and gooseberry pie. We had v. good sweet-sour pork, rice and crispy noodles. 27/- all told!! I'm writing all the details here because in years to come I shall read this and we shall say, '"Did we really pay so little? Fancy!"'

Our return was quite a marathon. We had decided to drive overnight rather than breaking our journey at a hotel, as we had done at vast expense on the way up. We got off the ferry at 7.15 and after bedding the kids down on eiderdowns, we set off. We stopped only once for a coffee from the thermos, finally arriving at Hildenborough at 3.30 a.m. We fell thankfully into bed.

Neal was actually looking forward to boarding school and we were able to see over much of it when we took his trunk over a few days before the start of term. A very pleasant assistant matron took us round, and we appreciated the *hot* showers in the cloakrooms, the central heating in the main house, which she assured us was often *too* hot, and the generally informal, happy atmosphere of the place. When the day came and we drove Neal over resplendent in his new uniform, we said goodbye hastily, having promised ourselves we wouldn't be the sort of parents who hang about waving and smiling, and he went off with Matron and another new boy. He looked as if he was about to burst with some emotion or other, but in truth we felt so happy about him that it was hard to feel really sorry, and we got letters from him saying how he liked it, with a comforting P.S. from the staff to say that he'd settled in well. He has been there four years now and will soon have to leave, and I must say we could not have chosen a finer school. Leslie can't get over the easy way boys chat to the Head, Mr Leakey, because in his day the Head was God Plus and you didn't often meet him, but if you did, you certainly wouldn't have a chatty conversation with him. I was relieved that there seemed to be none of the cruel bullying of new boys that Leslie can also vividly recall, with frightening initiation ceremonies to be gone through. He can recall a boy fainting on one occasion at his school, which at least had the effect of making authority step in.

We had planned to leave England just after Neal's half term. He had four days, so it was like old times to have him around again. With a family, I reckon that one more child is at least double two children in terms of noise and food consumed.

About a month before we left, Poppa had a coronary heart attack, and spent the rest of our leave in bed. We had a very worrying two days after it happened, which the doctor said were critical, but he pulled through and stayed on in the flat in Oxted, as he was actually too ill even to be taken in an ambulance. He got up and dressed for the first time the evening we called in at the flat to say goodbye, en route for the airport. It is always harrowing saying goodbye to parents when one is away for long tours, and I felt very lumpy as we drove off, with Mummy and Poppa waving from the window. I had a feeling I might never see him again and five months later he died very peacefully in hospital. How I hate the last few days of leave! Ann is as bad as I am about goodbyes and she is also susceptible to hymns. On our last Sunday we all went to the little church at Underriver for the Remembrance Day service. We sang 'Oh Valiant Hearts' and we both got very choked up. I was thinking especially of Poppa, quite apart from the usual emotions one experiences at this sort of service. We all went out into the churchyard to sing 'Abide with Me' (the coup de grace for me, I fear) by the war memorial, and as we sang, the first small flakes of snow came drifting down. The children had never seen it before!

Once we were on the plane, we settled down to while away the ten hours and were lucky that the plane was fairly empty so that we each had three seats to spread on to. In the end we all slept, and had an uneventful trip, except for a *faux pas* I made during the night. I woke up at one stage and fumbled my way to the lavatory. It was really very dark indeed and the little blue bulbs weren't much help as I bumbled back along the aisle, still half-asleep. I had difficulty in finding my place again but finally stumbled thankfully into what I thought was my row and flopped heavily down on top of an entirely strange sleeping gentleman. I leapt back with a mutter of apology and backed off hurriedly so that he wouldn't think my intentions were dishonourable. Then, feeling very silly and giggly, and dying to tell someone, I at last found my real place with great relief. It was hard to sleep and later, this time noting very carefully where I was, I went back to the toilet and spent a happy quarter of an hour anointing myself with all the tempting array of cosmetics that were laid out: hand cream, moisture cream, skin lotion, Cologne – I went through the lot, and finally wafted out in a cloud of mixed perfumes, grinning to myself since it seemed rather amusing to be sitting on a lavatory, thousands of feet up in the air and tearing along at 500 miles an hour, having a free rein with the cosmetics. No one was awake to share this joke either, and I eventually went back to sleep, half suffocated by my own expensive odour.

Dawn came at last, and the passengers stirred out of their unlovely sloth. This is the lowest ebb of air travel morale. The blinds are up, literally and metaphorically, and if you happen to be fairly alert, you can have fun watching your fellow passengers wake up bleary-eyed, hair rumpled and obviously with a foul taste in their mouths. They creep blindly to the toilet, where they hold up an impotent queue of fellow-sufferers while they too make liberal use of the lotions and cosmetics so generously provided. A friend of mine who was an air hostess once surprised an Asian lady stark naked in the toilet pouring a whole bottle of cologne over herself. I'm not surprised; the largesse of it all does tend to go to one's head.

Finally we started to come down; to me that is the most exciting part of air travel, when the engine-note changes into fine pitch (that's what Leslie tells me it's called) and you can feel that sinking feeling! We peered out to see our new home, miles of bush-dotted country, and there in the middle, the sprawling city of Nairobi.

It was overcast and drizzly, for November is the time of the 'short rains', but we were soon through Customs and being welcomed by the Hollands and David Pugh, our Number Two in Nairobi. Leslie and Stan stayed to see the heavy luggage through and the rest of us went back to the house full of anticipation. It stood in a quiet road, in just over an acre, surrounded by lovely trees, mostly eucalyptus and jacaranda, and was made of natural stone with a tiled roof. Huge picture windows looked on to a lawn sloping down to a stream that ran along the bottom of the garden. We had been warned never to touch the water, as bilharzia was known to exist there. This is a very nasty disease, transmitted via a certain kind of water snail, and was hard to detect and treat but could, if neglected, kill. It was hard to resist that stream; it tumbled down over a rocky outcrop, and bubbled past us so invitingly, just asking to be messed about in, dammed and fished from.

CHAPTER 13

Our 'pleasure life' in Nairobi

AT FIRST WE WERE GREETED politely by the dogs, who didn't seem to remember us, but gradually seemed dimly to recall that we had met before, and it was lovely so see them racing around, licking, wagging and looking so fit. We met our servants, Munguthi, who was cook and houseboy, and Joseph, who was gardener, washer-up and car cleaner. I hope it doesn't sound affected to say it was a great relief that there were only two of them! In Ceylon we had six, and I could write a whole book about that subject alone! We decided that the children, now eight, seven and four, were too old to have a nanny, so we didn't take on the Mitchell's but used to get a babysitter from the nearby old peoples' home. They were dear old ladies; we had three different ones in our 2½ years in Nairobi, although we didn't use them very often as we now had a television. This was wonderful, for I am not ashamed to admit that I adore my Findlay, Steptoe, Mogul, Bonanza and the rest, apart from some good local programmes.

We soon found that Nairobi was quite a sophisticated city, very cosmopolitan, with new skyscrapers going up all the time. Even these, however, couldn't spoil the beauty of the flowering trees and shrubs that grew profusely on all the many roundabouts and by the roads. At that time the jacaranda was out all over the city, trees of misty mauve, the pavements carpeted with their petals. Bougainvillea in every conceivable shade of red sprawled (but tidily) over wire pegged out to receive them. Purple plumbago, pink lilies, yellow alamanda, white gardenias – there they all were, making Nairobi one of the loveliest cities I have seen. It was hard to believe that the city started in the early 1900s as a glorified railway junction en route for Uganda. Then it was just a few tin shacks!

The climate is superb; being 5,453 feet up, it can be very cool, in the forties at night, and not hotter than about 80 in the daytime. The worst time of the year is in July, when it is constantly overcast without actually raining much. The altitude made itself felt; you felt your heart

Tess in the garden of the McMillan Road House in Nairobi, 1966.

thump if you ran, or even walked, uphill, and many people find they are very sleepy for the first week or two. It was a great delight to find we had a huge fireplace, which showed obvious signs of use. David Pugh told us that the Mitchells used it but that it was inclined to smoke. How we battled with that wretched chimney! Nothing would please it. We had it swept, we had it altered in shape to slope the smoke upwards, we used a wrought iron fire-box, we asked people's advice, but it took us seven months, on and off, to find the cause. It was *so* simple! In the end it was Leslie who suddenly wondered if the two exit holes on the top of the chimney were big enough to let out the smoke . . . A man went up the ladder and we found that the holes were even smaller than they seemed as the stone was sloped inwards. The man chipped away the stone, enlarged the holes, and we hopefully lit our fire and held our breath. To our joy, up went the smoke and none came billowing into the sitting-room! After that we had a crackling log-fire almost every night unless it was really too hot. Wood was very cheap (about £5 for a lorry-load) so we didn't have to skimp; one load lasted us six months. We sometimes used to remark on the strangeness of sitting before our fire watching *Dr Finlay's Casebook* and digesting our strawberries and cream. Hardly the Dark

Continent one expects! Actually, Nairobi is, in many ways, not the real Africa; there are so many places that are just like home. You could buy almost any flowers you cared to name: daffodils, roses, chrysanths., carnations, delphiniums, pansies, and not pay more than three shillings a bunch. Strawberries were available most of the year at about 2/6d. a punnet; cream was 2/6d. a half pint, asparagus 2/6d. a bundle, and in addition pawpaws, pineapples, apples, mulberries and avacados were available. The latter were 25 cents each when in season, which was 3d! Just before we left England, I had seen some small ones in a shop for 3/6d. each. Meat was also cheap; fillet steak was about 5/- a lb., but even so, people who had lived in Kenya a long time bemoaned the high prices of meat. The shops were full of imported goods, and for many months we would marvel at the amount of stuff you could buy and wonder how the poor luxury-starved Ceylonese would have reacted to such riches. There in Ceylon, you couldn't even import a car unless you were a Cabinet Minister, and the shops only sold exorbitantly-priced imported goods, usually at about twice their home price, or else a locally made substitute, which was all too often inferior. In Kenya, however, the local products (and there are many) are generally excellent: bacon, ham, cheese (I counted 14 different Kenyan varieties once in a supermarket, including Kenyan Blue, which is just like Danish Blue), butter, soups, jams, etc. All these crowd the shelves of the several supermarkets. One very large store in particular has a vast range of foods: wines, liquor, household goods, crockery, books, toys, clothes, stationery, medicines, and tools, all under one roof. At Christmas that store is jam-packed with people and has Father Christmas on hand, with a sack of free gifts for the children. You can understand when I say that I don't feel Nairobi represents the true African scene, although this sophistication is a growing part of life in Kenya today. However, if you want a glimpse of what I call the real Africa, you only have to drive for fifteen minutes into Nairobi National Park and there, on the windswept, sweeping Athi plains, dotted with thorn trees, you can watch a pride of lions lolling in the sun or see a rhino browsing, or you can visit the peaceful hippo pools and see the hippos blowing and splashing in the river. I cannot begin to describe the thrill of exploring the Park. Although it is small as parks go – only 44 square miles, compared with, say, Tsavo's 7000 square miles – it has so much to offer. If you are lucky, you may see all the more exciting big game except elephant. The park is not big enough to support these monsters, who are very destructive. In elephant country one can quickly notice the difference in the scenery, where there are many dead trees and cast-off branches, torn down by the animals in search of food.

All the same, I have seen in Nairobi Park, which is literally on the doorstep of the city, lion, cheetah, rhino, buffalo, giraffe, zebra, hyena, hippo, crocodile and about a dozen varieties of buck and gazelle. Of course, you are lucky if you see all these in one day. Sometimes the lion are just not to be found, although they tend to have their favourite haunts, and though leopard are to be seen in the Park, I have never been lucky. However, I have had the privilege of seeing a cheetah at the kill with her two fluffy cubs, and I have seen tiny lion cubs with their benevolent-looking mothers, and a friend and I once spent a nerve-wracking hour watching a lone lioness stalk two wart-hogs. Nearer and nearer she crept until she was so low in the long grass, we could only guess at her whereabouts. As the grazing warthogs, blissfully unaware of her, moved steadily nearer, the tension in our car grew unbearably. It was the awful pull of wanting to see a kill, yet feeling sorry for the victim. At long last, when we were like over-taut violin strings, the lioness exploded out of the grass a few yards from the warthogs. We jumped out of our wits, the warties pelted off and that blasted lioness *stood* and watched them! She had evidently just been playing, but we didn't appreciate it and we called her every name under the sun as we drove away, still muttering imprecations. On another exciting occasion I was on a lone visit to the Park. I had a spare morning and had decided to go on my own after looking over the fence to see if my neighbour was at home. Joan was a very keen Park-goer; it was she who had shared my frustration over the playful lioness. However, on this occasion I could see her car was gone, so off I went alone. Much later I was cruising along at the 20 m.p.h. of the Park when out of the corner of my eye I saw something odd happen in the long grass, where a Grant's Gazelle had been grazing. I braked hurriedly and could see something spotted, so with shaking hands I focussed the binoculars; no sign of the Grant's, but a glimpse of a spotted coat . . . Gibbering to myself with excitement, I drove on a few yards to a level bit and turned off the road. As I bumped along through the whistling-thorn bushes, I was praying that whatever it was wouldn't go away. I was in the new Renault 16, and poor L. would have had a fit at its treatment, but suddenly I found her: a beautiful female cheetah, panting as she rested by the dead gazelle. She dragged it on further, then stopped by a bush and I almost fainted with delight as two furry cubs tottered up to investigate. Shaking with excitement, I sat about 20 feet away and watched as she lay down, taking no interest in her prey. The babies tumbled about her but seemed too small to eat meat. They had the very long fluff on their backs that makes them look as if they are wearing a badly-fitting fur coat! As they get older, new short fur grows, until the long fluff is only over the shoulders.

Some people criticise Nairobi Park and feel that the animals are so used to humans that they don't count as being wild. Certainly some visitors show incredible stupidity in the way they lean out of open windows a few yards away from a pride of lions. I have heard of objects being thrown at the sleeping animals to 'liven them up' for a good snap. Certainly it isn't much fun to see your lions by joining twenty other cars parked in a circle round the pride; all too often they are in long grass, and if they lie flat, as they so often do, you cannot see more than a twitching tail. One of the nicest sights Joan and I ever saw was a pride of lion walking down the road ahead of us. There were two mums, one with two very small cubs about two or three months old. The other had three older ones, six or seven months, and there was one auntie. They all ambled along, with us creeping behind at a respectful distance, as we didn't want to harass them. After the first few minutes, the smallest cubs stopped gambolling and fooling about and got a bit tired. At intervals, the grown-ups would stop and scan the scenery – for game, I suppose. Immediately the footsore babies would sink down for a rest, only to stagger up after a few minutes to move on. The older cubs pulled the grown-ups' tails, including Auntie's, and played with a stick. They were very carefree. At long last they were led off the road, and we hoped the babies would get a rest. Later we found they had walked about 1¹/₂ miles, no mean feat for a small cub. We had been joined by another car and we watched jealously in case they chivvied the pride. One becomes very possessive about 'one's own' lions. One doesn't want to share them, and if someone else turns up, they are very much on sufferance. To find some lions entirely on your own, without cheating by asking a ranger or by just joining a circle of other cars, is the most satisfying thing I know. Once, on my own, I found three lionesses dozing right by the road. I parked about eight feet away and sat for fifteen minutes watching and repressing a desire to get out and tickle an upturned tummy. Lions are very sociable and if one meets another, they rub cheeks in a most touching manner, and they are most easy-going with small cubs. You have to remind yourself that they would be very different if you got out of the car!

You mustn't think Nairobi Park is a roaring mass of lions. Don't be like a friend of mine, fresh from England, who, seeing a notice, 'Beware of Lion', immediately wound up the window and peered wildly out; she was most disappointed not to see one! Sometimes you can meet them on the road. I once had six walk past the car a yard away. Again I was on my own, twittering away to myself and taking pictures madly. Most of the time they will lie in some inaccessible spot, and you daren't risk bumping the car over bad ground or ground that's too wet. I have been bogged down twice in the Park and it's no fun. Wet black cotton soil, which, with red dust, makes up the Park terrain, is exactly like glue mixed with cocoa powder, with the clinging tenacity of nougat – a beastly mixture. I have had the humiliation of being towed out by a Parks jeep on both occasions, and both times cheetah were responsible for our plight! Luckily the Park is small, but there have been some nasty cases of people stuck in Tsavo for days.

One of our favourite places was the Mokoyeti Gorge. Here you are allowed to get out of your car and look down into the river that runs below; usually there are waterbuck or perhaps a crocodile or giraffe below, but the main attraction is the charming rock hyrax that can often be seen sunning themselves a few yards below, lolling on the warm rocks in abandoned positions. A hyrax is like a very large guinea pig, about a foot long, but those who ought to know say his nearest relative is the elephant, due to the formation of his feet. Anyone who saw the film of *Born Free* will recall Patti the hyrax, and I always had designs on the Park ones; I did so want one as a pet! They are very restless animals, incapable of lying still for more than a minute. One will upset a whole group by walking on top of them to find a 'better 'ole' and that sets them all off, nudging and pushing and arguing; it was a wonder no one tumbled off into the ravine! They are *always* scratching too. Joy Adamson reckons it's just grooming, not fleas; they certainly seem to get great satisfaction from it.

Giraffes were great favourites of mine; they are so quiet and gentle and such an elegant shape. It was two giraffes staring so intently into the grass that made me alert for the cheetah that I saw at the kill. They watched aloofly; killing is part of life to them, 'as long as it's not me, no one cares,' is the attitude. Animals know when a lion is hunting and I've seen gazelles grazing happily near a pride. As long as they can see what is going on, they don't worry. They are a good example to us humans in the way they all mingle. You can often see zebra, Tommies, Grant's, kongoni, wildebeeste and ostrich all mixed up; they just ignore each other and get about their own business.

I could go on for pages about the joys of the Park, but most of it has been said before in the many books about Africa which fill my bookshelves. Perhaps a little less has been written about the unique Animal Orphanage that is by the Main Gate into the Park. It was quite small originally, but in the three years we have known it, it has been given new grounds and better facilities for coping with the vast numbers of orphaned wild babies and unwanted pets and mascots. I used to spend many happy hours there. Sometimes I could catch Bobby Cade, who was the boss there until he died in 1967. He would talk fascinatingly about his charges, and would sometimes take me behind the scenes and show me a few of his special pets. He was not fond of lions, however; one night he was on television with some tiny baby hedgehogs, and he said he had more satisfaction bringing them up and watching them than he ever got from lions. One day when I went to the Orphanage he was in a terrible rage. In the night, some wild Park lions had roamed up and down the Orphanage boundary wire and had terrorised a lot of the smaller, timid types of antelope. One poor Tommy had leapt the four-foot high fence and was found at the petrol station nearby. Another had battered itself to death on the fence in its panic, but the worst hit was a pair of eland calves, of which Mr Cade was particularly proud. One was just getting to its feet for the first time that morning; it was terribly shaky, and covered in cuts and bruises from running blindly into the fence. The other lay unmoving and in spite of the vet's attention, it died next day. Cade was in a frightful rage and was all for poisoning every lion in the Park. 'They've got the whole of the rest of the bloody Park, why do they come here?' he demanded.

Apart from boarding odd pets like spider monkeys, bushbabies and otters for absent owners, the Orphanage gets given many 'outgrown' pets such as cheetah, leopard, baboon and chimps. This leads me on to Sebastian, without whom the Orphanage would be nothing . . .

Sebastian is a chimp of great personality and verve. He is now about six years old, I think, which is adult for this species, and correspondingly unreliable. When I first saw him, he was in a big pen tethered by a running chain, which was padlocked to a collar on his neck. He knew exactly how far he could reach and devised many games to entertain his fans, for there was always a crowd round him, which he adored. He preferred to have a preponderance of Africans in his audience; experience had shown that they shrieked the loudest when he threw things at them! He would warm up first with a few standing jumps, all his hair on end, screaming excitedly. Once sure he had everyone's attention, he would pick up an old sack used as bedding and proceed to stroll up and down, peering beneath his brows, until suddenly the sack would be hurled over the four-foot fence, and those nearest would duck or run. Sometimes he would score a bullseye and the victim would sportingly return the sack for another try. Sometimes he would hurl pieces of wood, but this was not encouraged. In spite of this, he regularly dismantled his house for ammunition. We often gave him presents and he was most grateful. Tessa's old straw hat and broken pair of sunglasses were both worn with great gusto, albeit upside-down, and an old lipstick case made him really sit down and examine it. He found that by sticking in his finger, he could get out a small amount of lipstick, which he gleefully put on his fingers and toes. I was interested to notice that when I gave him a pencil, he immediately picked up an old piece of brown paper and scribbled on it. Mr Cade used to bemoan the fact that he had no time to spare to spend with Sebastian; he was very teachable. Fans used to buy him ice cream, and he always started off using the wooden spoon; but after a few delectable mouthfuls, greed would get the better of him and he would lick out the rest. He would hold out his tin mug for his milk and drink decorously, and he adored a cigarette, lying on his back, legs crossed, puffing away like the addict he was!

Another of Sebastian's games was the highjacking of cameras, glasses, scarves – in fact any object that a foolish member of the public chose to risk by leaning too far over the fence. Bobby Cade used to say glumly that the fences were to protect the animals rather than the reverse, for people were often incredibly foolish in their familiarity with Sebastian and I am ashamed to admit that I was one of them. One day Margaret Holland and I went to visit the Orphanage and found a large crowd round Sebastian. He was in grand form and highly delighted with himself, having snatched a pair of rather good dark glasses from a spectator. He knew perfectly well that great, if unobtrusive, efforts were being made to get them back. A Game Scout tried to cajole him with a bottle of orange fizz, indicating it was a fair swop for the glasses. However, the wily chimp refused to barter, and even the ruse of offering two bottles merely caused him to transfer the glasses to one of his feet, which were as good as hands. How the glasses remained intact I'll never know, for he frequently put them on his nose and raced about gloating, and if he put them down for a moment, he covered them with a foot. He would even let you hold the glasses as he lay near you on his back, languidly allowing people to tickle his toes, which he loved, but would not release his grip. Margaret leant right over, holding them, cajoling him, and so did I. Later I realised how foolish we were; he could have so easily pulled us in. It was only a few months later, when we were on leave, that Margaret wrote to say that he had suddenly turned on a Game Scout who was feeding him and had mauled him badly. After that, plans were made for a new and stronger cage for him, and it was almost complete when someone noticed that the steel-wire cable on to which Sebastian's running chain was attached was almost frayed through. Immediately a race against time began to finish the cage, and the papers were full of the story of Sebastian's transfer. He had to be drugged for the move and everyone had a very lively time shooting him with an anaesthetic dart. When a bullseye was at last scored, he snatched the dart from his rump with a shriek of rage and hurled it back at his assailant. Then he went berserk for a few minutes until the drug finally took effect. He woke up a few hours later in his handsome new cage, but the whole experience had affected him deeply and it took him weeks to get over it. Denis Kearney had been one of those present at the darting, and if he went near Sebastian afterwards, he was screamed and raged at, and so was anyone who wore a khaki jacket like the one worn by Mr Monks, the vet who had actually shot him. Apart from this, he seemed unhappy in his new surroundings when I went to see him a few weeks after the move. The new cage was some distance from the Orphanage, on the site of the new extension, so unless people knew he was there or specially asked to be shown the way, he had far fewer visitors. He still wore his collar, but was now free in a large steel-barred cage, with a big bedroom, swings and all you would think he could wish for. However, there he sat, looking sad, and only cheered up when the Assistant Warden brought him an ice.

'We're rather sucking up to him to get his confidence back,' he told me as he handed the ice to Sebastian. 'It really did affect him mentally; we got quite worried after the move.' He went on to tell me of Sebastian's hatred of Monks and Kearney. It is very hard to keep such an intelligent animal occupied and happy, and it was very obvious that Sebastian pined for his public. I believe that captive gorillas suffer from the same tendency to boredom, which, after they grow up, cannot be helped by human contact because of their untrustworthy tempers.

However, Sebastian was not entirely cast down because some months later we read that he had broken out and had had a lovely spree! The clever thing had prised apart the bars, which must have been over $3/4"$ thick, using his swing as a lever. He had then, according to a gleeful report in the press, galloped across the road to the Langata Cemetery where there was a funeral in progress. Luckily he ignored the interment and shinned up a tree in another part of the cemetery, where he hurled abuse and sticks at his pursuers. I rather think he had to be darted again before he was recaptured; he was far too wily to be trapped. The latest news I heard of him was a recent report in the paper that a marriage was being arranged between Sebastian and Sisi, a younger female chimp who also lived in the Orphanage; I should think he will make a pretty incorrigible husband! I must say, I am very fond of chimps and gorillas, but I am not at all keen on monkeys and they are one of the few animals I would never have as a pet; they are too uncertain tempered for my liking (though Gerald Durrell would probably not agree with me), and can bite really hard. The only animals I disliked in Nairobi Park were the baboons. These wander all over the Park in big packs, and if you stop the car they will jump onto the bonnet and explore. Foolish visitors feed them, little realising the danger (perhaps they have never seen a baboon yawn; they have huge pointed canine teeth like a great dog) and despite notices forbidding feeding. The result is that the animals lose all fear of humans and will turn nasty when food is refused. Some had to be shot when they became over-familiar and someone was bitten, and now there is always a ranger down at the Hippo Pools, partly to stop people from feeding the monkeys and baboons. I also harbour a grudge against one huge old male who pinched most of our breakfast one morning. We had parked by the Mokoyeti Gorge, and had spread out the food on a rock when Sarah cried out from behind me, 'Look out, a baboon.' I was about to tell her not to be silly, as I had never seen one in this area, when I turned round in time to see the wretched beast simply stuffing our bread and butter into his mouth; the kids fled to the safety of the can and in my rage, I flung the nearest missile at the enemy, which happened to be an orange. It missed, of course, but he followed it into the bushes and a few rocks hurled after him persuaded him he was far from welcome at our picnic. I had been horribly conscious of my new binoculars, lying within a few inches of his grasping hands, and had frightful visions of them being grabbed, carried off into the bush and lost forever. We hastily gathered up the remains of our meal, to a husbandly obbligato of: 'I told you it wasn't a very good place to eat, but you wouldn't listen.' Another thing that does not endear baboons to me is a series of photos I saw in an exhibition in Nairobi. It shows a great male baboon busy devouring a baby gazelle. They are believed to be the first photos of this kind. I have read somewhere that they will crack open the skull to get at the brains . . . Now perhaps you can understand how even such an ardent animal-lover as I has an aversion to baboons. The babies are quite sweet, though, riding on Mamma's back in a jaunty fashion and fooling about and teasing their elders and betters until they get a cuff over the ear which sends them screaming back to Mum. They have pathetically sad, wrinkled faces when very young – quite human, really.

I have mentioned that Nairobi Park has no elephants. We had been in Kenya eight months before we saw any of these wonderful beasts. Neal came out for the summer holidays, and we drove 300 miles down to stay by the sea at Mombasa. Nowadays the road is all tarmac, but three years ago, about half was still sandy track and it was quite an adventure if it had rained. You were liable to get bogged down, or even if it was dry, a flying stone could smash your windscreen or a puncture or two could hold you up for hours. A lot of the road passed through Tsavo Park, which it divides in two, East and West. It is on this stretch that you can often see elephants and we were lucky to see a total of seven that day. They stood by the side of the road, rightly ignoring us entirely, with that mournful look that even happy elephants seem to have, stuffing grass into their mouths, and they were *bright* orangey-red! It was a shattering enough experience to view one's first elephant from a few yards away, but for them to be that unbelievable colour was just too much! The soil in that part is, of course, the cause, because the elephants love a mud-bath, and don't bother to rinse off. It is the brightest, ruddiest, bricky red you could ever imagine, just *not* an elephant colour, but of course you do get used to it in the end. Now the Mombasa road is all tarmac, but you can still see the elephants as they amble across if they feel like it, and there are thrilling notices at intervals: 'Beware of Elephants'. For the life of me, I can't begin to understand how anyone could want to kill one except in an emergency, and one effect of living in Kenya has been to turn me against big game hunting more than ever before. Thank goodness the days of wholesale slaughter for fun seem to be over, and anyone who wants to come and kill our game has to pay a hefty sum for the 'privilege'. More people seem to prefer photography or just watching, and the tourist trade here is a huge earner of foreign currency. Much has already been written on the importance of conservation, and I don't propose to add much, except this: I am horrified at the large numbers of shops in Kenya that are full of skins and trophies ... I cannot believe these vast numbers are all legitimately shot, and it is this thought that prevents me from ever buying anything made of game skin or horn; anyone who has seen films and pictures, or even read, of the frightful tortures inflicted by snares on animals must know what I mean, but when I tell people why I refuse to buy trophies, they are most surprised and say they never thought of it that way. If only everyone would boycott these gruesome objects, the cruelty would be considerably reduced. I suppose *someone* must buy a table lamp made from a single zebra foot and hoof, or it wouldn't be produced. Wastepaper baskets of elephants' feet, earrings from the horns of dik-dik, which are the tiniest, daintiest little antelopes of all, cigarette cases of elephant's ear skin, and of course, bags and hats of leopard and cheetah – there they are and shop after shop is full of them, a depressing sight for anyone who pauses to think of the implications. Occasional letters appear here in the press, but still the shops are full. I suppose one day man may change his selfish and destructive attitude. Let's hope it won't be too late if and when it ever happens.

CHAPTER 14

A shaggy dog show,
television and bad news

POOR SKIPPER! She seems to have slipped out of the story but she soon pops into prominence again! In July, 1966, the S.P.C.A. held its Shaggy Dog Show at the Kennel Club grounds. This is an annual event which gives a chance for non-pedigree dogs to shine, so you can imagine how much we looked forward to it for our two. The class I was most interested in was the Veteran, for dogs over seven years. Skip was 12, Pingo 7, so we decided to enter both. Great preparations went on and both reluctant competitors were bathed. Skipper was combed until she was a fluffy bundle. It was rather a dull, cool day when we arrived in the morning, and we had a picnic lunch under the trees in the interval. The Veteran Class was late in the afternoon, but we put them in for various other classes: The Curliest Tail, the Shortest Nose, the Bandiest Legs, etc, for the 1/- entry fee for each dog went to the S.P.C.A. The classes were judged by various local celebrities, including Michaela Denis, who lives in Nairobi, and Mr Slade, the Speaker of the House.

At last, when all the children had had a turn in the ring, it was my turn, and with Leslie leading Ping, we walked sedately round the ring before the two vets who were judging. There were many entries but even while trying to be unprejudiced, I knew Skipper looked superb. She trotted jauntily round, tail curled and pluming gaily, her white legs dazzling, her black fur shining from my shampoo and Estolan. In the end a black Border collie with two children got first. He was a year older than Skip and in good condition, though not combed enough, I thought, and Skip got second, a blue rosette and some dog-food, and we were very thrilled. Ping was not placed and had taken strong exception to the judge looking at her teeth. She had a very good idea of how she wanted to use them, and Leslie had to open her mouth for her. She has never liked being mauled by strangers, even well-meaning ones. Skip got a lot of attention from people, who wanted to know what she was, and she met Michaela Denis. Furthermore I had won my heat with Ping in the egg and spoon, so we were well content and looked forward to next year.

As soon as we were settled in Nairobi, I began to take soundings to find out whether I could take up broadcasting again. There was also the tantalising thought of television. After badgering the right people, I managed to get a television test, which was quite an education, apart from the frightfulness of seeing yourself caught unawares on the monitor-screen. I had a yen to do some advertising, so there I sat in my best dress clutching a script, while Sikh cameramen and other technicians milled about busily. Unfortunately I had been singularly unintelligent about my makeup. Although I was aware that the bright arc-lights killed all but the heaviest makeup, I chose to wear a pale pink lipstick that matched my dress. The result was a sudden glimpse of a huge-chinned, deathly pale self on a monitor, looking as though I had been dead by drowning for some weeks, It was most demoralising. Anyhow, everyone was so kind and helpful, I eventually got through two commercials, which they said charitably were 'Very good, very good,' and when I left, I realised it wasn't the easiest job. Anyhow, nobody ever asked me to do them a commercial again, though I had tests with two other kind people who were in advertising. This time it was sound only, and I preferred to be heard but not seen. Nothing came of them, however. All the same, I did realise both ambitions: to be on T.V. and on the air. I volunteered (you can't keep a good man down) for a quiz show on television, and the first time I won 30/- and had to go back the next week, when I was unfortunately beaten! The broadcast was great fun. Each Christmas and New Year, V.O.K. lends its studios and staff to a charitable organisation to raise money for the blind of Kenya by playing records that listeners phone in and request, pledging money for each record. People are incredibly generous and will pay from 10/- to five pounds to hear their choice. Volunteers work through Christmas night and New Year's Eve to keep the turntables busy, and over a thousand pounds was collected last year. In addition to records, kind people donate stuff for auction, anything from a prize bull, a case of whisky, a trip to Treetops or a night out with a blonde – anything goes! People phone in their bids and after a time the article is knocked down to the highest bidder. The fun is too often marred by people with a warped sense of humour who phone bids in the name of some unsuspecting person. One year a car was knocked down to poor Mr Nanji, a well-known business man, quite without his knowledge, and though he sportingly paid part of the price, it meant a loss to the blind. 1966 saw the 'Ring Us Up' Programme on television for the first time. It was an amazing success and I sat entranced till past one a.m. until I really couldn't keep my eyes open any longer. My small bit was half an hour's disc jockeying on Boxing Day. It was great fun, but I had to have Hassan Mazoa, one of V.O.K's announcers, to help me, as you were expected to twiddle all the right knobs as well as put on the records and tapes. I just read out the message and who it was from and for, and Hassan did all the work, but Leslie taped it and it sounds quite professional.

The children also had their finger in the television pie. There was a good programme called 'Art for the Young' every Monday, run by a young man called Michael Croydon. Each week he gave the children in the studio an art lesson and gave the viewing children a subject to send in for next week. Each week the best would be shown on the screen and discussed. Sarah and Tessa had their pictures in on two occasions and Neal once, which was a great thrill. Later, the programme was altered slightly and was taken over by Mr Kareithi, whose daughter went to the same school as Sarah, and they managed to get themselves on to the programme. We burst with pride at home watching them hard at work with their paints under the bright lights.

Later, they also appeared on another children's programme, and took with them Skipper and Henry Cuddles, a hamster we had bought for Christmas. I had decided against Ping appearing, as she has a much more nervous temperament than the equable Skipper, and she would have hated the many people, lights and strange surroundings of the television studio. However, Sarah, Tessa, Skip and Henry all behaved excellently. The girls each held an animal and were interviewed about care and history. We couldn't find quite so much to tell about Henry, but many of the children in the studio had never seen a hamster before and were most interested, and they liked hearing that Skipper was twelve years old and had travelled over 7,000 miles with us on our different postings about the world. One thing about having a long-haired dog is that it is so rewarding to beautify, and when Skip is bathed and combed, she looks terrific. You don't get quite the same effect with Ping, with her short hair, but her white coat certainly looks sparkling after a hated bath!

I recently found a picture of Skipper taken in 1966 when we were collecting for the S.P.C.A. flag day. She looks marvellous and although I cannot remember the amount we collected that year, I have a note for the next year that a combination of Skip, myself, Sarah and Tessa collected just over eleven pounds in a morning in Wabera St., which is a busy place in the city. It was very interesting watching the prospective victim's expression when he realised you were there; some people would hurriedly cross the road to avoid you, some stared fixedly ahead and marched past unseeing, others smiled uneasily and muttered they had no change. Other stalwarts would actually come up without being asked, and I was most touched at the many not-so-prosperous Africans who gave us a few cents very willingly. I always enjoy flag selling; after the first rather embarrassed few 'touches', I get into my stride, and it is pleasant to meet people and chat to them. Very few are actually nasty, though one man said he didn't like animals and refused us, but at least it is more honest than the person who 'has no change'. There seemed to be a chronic shortage of spare coppers that Saturday morning. On the other hand, one lady, with my permission, took the girls upstairs to her nearby office, and gave them some money because she really didn't have the necessary with her in her bag. Skipper came in for the usual attention, and I freely confess that I burst with pride on these occasions; she is such a patient and good tempered little dog, you can take her anywhere and know she will lie quietly under your chair or is safe to be patted by the smallest child. The only occasion she has ever tried to bite was when I mated her to Jygmeh for a third time in one heat to try to ensure some results. It was obviously painful and she twisted her head and nipped me on the hand very mildly. Otherwise she will growl thunderously if the children try to take liberties, such as removing a favourite bone or ball, but she has never even growled at me.

April, 1966 was an eventful but sad month. Neal came out for his first holiday in Kenya, and we had booked to stay in Tsavo Park at Aruba, where there was a choice of tents or small huts (called 'bandas' out here). We chose tents, much to the childrens' glee, but the day before we left we had a phone call from England from Mummy to say that Daddy had died in his sleep in hospital the night before. He had only been there a few days, and we all felt it was better this way. He would have hated the life of an invalid. He was a very gentle, self-effacing person, and his deafness made him shy. Moreover, he hated to give trouble to people. It seemed very hard to take in the news; nothing changed in Nairobi; our life went on and the holiday helped to stop the children from thinking too much about Grandpa, whom they loved. I was selfishly thankful that Ann and Chris were there to help Mummy, and I am still grateful that I missed the strain of the funeral. I know I would have broken down. Dear Ann wrote so understandingly, and they all knew at home how helpless we felt, but Poppa of all people would have been *horrified* at the very idea of anyone flying from Africa for his funeral. He was cremated, which I like, and his ashes lie at Worth under a rosebush called Peace that he was fond of. He loved gardening, and I think he would have preferred the spacious lawns, trees, and beautiful roses of the Memorial Garden to a weedy grave in some dreary churchyard. Certainly I don't intend to be buried. Ideally I should like my body to go for medical research and to have no funeral, at least not one with my friends and relatives; I feel that the burden of bereavement is sufficient without adding the strain of a funeral, and in fact I have written out a deposition to say I want no one at my cremation but the undertaker. When I was about 12 and kept hens, I felt a good way to dispose of my ashes would be to make them into a dustbath for hens; I still feel this isn't such a bad idea . . .

Just after Easter, we had a letter from Leslie's sister Bill to say that his mother, coming out of church on Easter Day, had tripped and fractured the neck of the femur. Mother was then a very active and independent person of over eighty, living alone in her flat in Dulwich, so the sudden change to the life of an invalid hit her very hard. Tragically, eleven months later she had another fall and broke the other femur, and now lives with Bill near St Albans in what used to be the school of Ayot St Lawrence, Shaw's home. She cannot walk without support now, but has her own rooms on the ground floor and goes twice a week to the hospital for therapy.

They say troubles come in threes, and they did in this case. My sister's son Geoff fell out of the treehouse at the start of the holidays and broke his arm. Poor Ann, she must have been glad when the holidays were over and Geoff's arm came out of plaster at last.

Our stay at Aruba, in spite of the circumstances, was as pleasant as it could be. We had two well-equipped tents overlooking the dam, which had been created to ensure a good supply of water for the animals. There was a main building, with a sitting-room, dining-room and a bar, and it was run by a pleasant young couple who had plenty of good 'game' stories to tell.

We were amazed at the shyness of all the animals in Tsavo. We had been spoilt by Nairobi Park and we felt rather insulted when the Tsavo animals turned tail and ran while we were still a long way off in the car. However, with a ranger to guide us, we saw some new animals to add to our list. One of the oddest was the gerenuk, which is a sort of antelope with an extraordinary elongated neck and huge eyes. It sometimes stands on its hind legs to reach out-of-the-way leaves as it browses. We saw several, and when one of them *did* stand up, just as the book said, we were thrilled. We also saw oryx, another antelope, very tall, with a handsome striped face and long, straight, scimitar horns. We saw no lions but lots of elephant and a rhino. It was just after we had seen him, early one morning when we were out on our own, that we went over a hump on a bridge, and stuck firmly halfway. Out we all got, against the rules, but we all had to push. We all pushed and gave advice, and still we stuck and it began to rain. We wondered if the rhino was coming our way, and we also wondered if any cars were likely to come our way. The river beneath our bridge was dirty and fast flowing and we hoped the bridge would hold and that the rain would stop – my goodness, how we hoped! In the end Leslie rallied us all, we had an extra child with us, so there were six to push, and after what seemed a very long half-hour, we got off the bridge and drove back to a late breakfast. That afternoon the kids were invited to go fishing, and Neal and Sarah went off in a small boat with the manager and a friend and, to our surprise, came back later with three large catfish, which looked very bristly and inedible but which I was assured were delicious! They were about two feet long, horribly slimy, and still twitching in spite of having been hit on the head; I find it most unnerving the way some creatures appear to be alive when they can't possibly be; apart from the legendary chicken, snakes can writhe and wiggle for about fifteen minutes after you have thoroughly killed them, and as I quite like snakes, it worries me. I always seem to like the creatures no one else loves. I have a soft spot for vultures, hyenas and toads as well as snakes. I really ought to find out more about which are harmless, because in common with most people in Mombasa, where we now live, I kill snakes just in case, but I don't like doing it.

Nairobi has a very efficient Snake Park run by Mr James Ashe, and I have spent many happy hours there listening to him talking about his charges. Once I asked him if we could handle one, as the children had never done so and I wanted them to dispel the old myth of 'they're slimy and cold,' which so many people trot out when you mention snakes. He brought out a small python, and it made me think of an occasion in Chittagong when I ruined a snake charmer's reputation by stroking his python! He was a good showman and had a gaping crowd round him one day in our compound. I steered clear of the cobra he had, though commonsense told me he wasn't the type to risk his neck with a full-fanged poisonous snake, but the python was a different proposition. Anyone ought to know that they are non-poisonous; they kill by constriction. I picked it up, I think, to a horrified hissed intake of breath from the bystanders. You can get a very similar reaction from an African if you wave a chameleon under his nose. Apparently there is a story that when God made the world, he told the chameleon to fetch everyone with a black skin to bathe in a pool that would make them white. He took so long about it that when the Africans arrived, there was only enough water left to whiten their soles and palms, and they have harboured a grudge ever since. However, this tale, which I hope I have told right, hardly accounts for the actual fear most Africans show for the chameleon. It is a rather menacing figure if roused, with its ability to change its colour before your eyes, and the ones we get down in Mombasa have an inflatable throat; when at rest, it is plain green, but if the animal is picked up, it opens its mouth and hisses and blows out its throat to show handsome dark red stripes. This is its sole means of defence, which is one reason for my always stopping the car to help one across the road, as I mentioned earlier in this book. They are often ungrateful and hiss peevishly, and occasionally I wonder guiltily if they were actually going anywhere special, and whether by interfering, I have messed up their plans, but they look so helpless and ponderous as they stride majestically across, that I feel I have to save them from possible death. There aren't too many drivers about who worry.

Talking about drivers reminds me of my own experiences behind the wheel. When Leslie and I got engaged, Mother very sweetly gave me a series of driving lessons as a present. I spent several weeks lurching round Marylebone in second gear, gradually improving until the day came for my test. It was right out at Stratford (London, not Upon Avon) in a pretty sleazy area. I was absolutely terrified and also suffered from being overclad in a tweed suit with a top coat over it. What with nerves, I sweated frightfully and did awful things. At one stage I was told to turn right and was about to do so when another pupil from my driving school who was under test emerged from the turning and stalled dismally. I sat there full of sympathy. My instructor had told me that particular examiner was very strict, so there I stayed, half across the road, sympathetically watching my fellow-sufferer sort out his gears and get moving again. Suddenly I realised I had a hooting queue behind me, and I hastily moved out of the way. My examiner just sat breathing stertorously, never *saying* anything except 'Turn right here', or 'Stop here'. It was most unnerving. I wanted to talk to him all the time, to explain why I was changing gear here, or slowing down there, in case he was not fully appreciating what a careful driver I was being. There was an embarrassing moment at a zebra crossing when I suddenly decided to let a woman pushing a pram go across; I was a bit close really, and had to brake hard and the poor man almost went through the windscreen. Anyhow, in the end, as I'd suspected, he failed me and I didn't really blame him. Mother was very understanding and stood me another six lessons, and after a few months I went through it all again, and when we finally came to a stop, I felt I had done better. However, the examiner told me off for hooting at some children playing in the street. 'It was damnably rude,' he told me surprisingly, but by this time I saw he had taken out the yellow form that meant 'Pass', so I nodded sycophantically and agreed with him all the time, watching that bit of paper out of the corner of my eye in case he changed his mind. After all this trouble and expense, I was allowed to drive very seldom in the next twelve years because Leslie hates being driven, especially by me, and is the original Back Seat Driver. I only had two short attempts, once with the old station waggon on the Isle of Skye, and once in Chittagong with the Jeep. However, when we heard we were posted to Kenya, everyone told me I *must* drive myself there, so I took a refresher course, chugging round Colombo's back streets in an old Morris with a scared lady instructor. There was one small incident that tended to sap my confidence in my tutor. It happened as we were going round and round a quiet residential square. There was another learner there in a Mini, and at one stage, we parked rather close behind her. The Mini's instructor hopped out, came over to us and angrily told me my instructor had no business to let me come so close to a learner. She then added disparagingly that she knew my instructor, that she was not properly qualified, and that she herself had worked at the same school and intended to tell the proprietor what she thought of my teacher. We drove off in high dudgeon, but in spite of this I found I had a confidence now I had never had before, and I was soon able to drive our Anglia. This gave me a wonderful chance to get my own back on a driver from whom Ginny and I had suffered for years. He was really awful. We did try to get him sacked, but he was terribly servile and the third wife who shared him with us liked the way he carried her parcels and generally mopped and mowed, so we had to put up with him or not go out. One afternoon he turned up to take us to the Swimming Club as usual, and when I said, 'I'll drive,' he nearly dropped dead. He sat crouched beside me hanging on for dear life, muttering 'Mind, lady, there is a car...' 'Look out, a lorry', and wincing all the time, although I drove far better than he ever did. At least I've never reversed straight out into a main road without looking, as he did once! It was a supreme moment for me, and I retailed the details with glee to Ginny. Actually, we did once have a worse driver when he was off sick. Ginny and I both wanted to go shopping one day so Leslie lent us a lorry driver from the factory. Afterwards, pale and wild-eyed, Ginny and I compared notes about our experiences and decided we were lucky to be alive. He was very old and wizened and drove peering through screwed-up eyes as though he wasn't seeing too clearly... His use of gears was sporadic. One took off with a jerk each time that almost dislocated one's neck. He seemed unaware of any other vehicles on the road and Ginny became deeply suspicious when he went straight over a red light. I mentioned to Leslie that it might be a good idea if he had a check-up, and some time later we were told he was half-blind and had been demoted from lorries to little trolleys that zoomed about the factory loaded with tea-chests; I suppose that was less dangerous than a lorry, but not much.

I have found that driving in the East, or East Africa even, is a hazardous business due to the widespread belief in the magic of the hand signal. This manifests itself in a huge variety of signals, varying from those taught by the numerous driving schools to those invented by enterprising drivers off their own bat. There are many variations, from the straight one-finger point, 'I am going Right', to the graceful wave up and down, 'I am slowing'. However, it may also mean 'I am going right if I can get round this handcart'. There is also the limp hand that just hangs, and your job is to guess its meaning: right, left, slow, cigarette ash, cool breeze or just not room for it in the car (not surprising when you see some families: there's Dad at the wheel, intrepid man, then Mum, Auntie, Gran, Grandpa, and a host of children. These are always Asians, who love 'togetherness'.) The one thing all hand signals have in common is the owner's implicit belief that once he has completed this rite, nothing can touch him. He can cross under your bonnet, stop on sixpence, slow down for a pal, but he reckons he'll be all right as long as he's signalled. Mind you, it is only a small minority who *do* signal; most drivers here just *go*, and if they do cut it a bit fine and you blast at them self-righteously, they smile infuriatingly and may even wave at you. Very few seem to use indicators, and I really do think they ought to be tested on both sorts of signals instead of hand only. You need both hands on the wheel, I think. I do try hard to remember I was a scared learner once as I sit impatiently behind some novice at a junction waiting for him to sort out his gears, but I do feel they ought not to be allowed in traffic until they at least know bottom from top gear.

CHAPTER 15

The case of the dog
that barked in the night

ONE OF THE FIRST QUESTIONS I was asked about Nairobi when we heard we were going to live there was: 'Are there any pi-dogs?' In Ceylon and India I was so often harrowed by the plight of the strays that haunted dustbins, shops and markets, skinny and unwanted. I was highly delighted to hear that there were none in Nairobi, but no one told me that there was a far worse aspect to the sophisticated city and its suburbs, and that was the large number of stray dogs that had owners who couldn't be bothered to keep them under control. This manifested itself in two ways, both distressing. One was the problem of barking dogs at night, the other was the vast numbers of dogs (and cats) run over on the roads. Hardly a week would pass without my seeing some pathetic corpse in the gutter. Often no one even bothered to move the body to the side and it would lie for as much as two days, with cars carefully driving round it. Often, they had been nice looking dogs. I recall a young Alsatian pup that lay for 48 hours on a very busy road. Another time it was a Labrador, and twice a daschund. If the dog had a collar, I used to stop the car to see if it had a name on it, but they never did. People weren't that interested.

The extent of the stray dog menace was brought home to us just after our arrival in Nairobi, when Ping came in season. In Ceylon, we spent our last tour in a house that had a walled garden, which was such a help in keeping out unwanted suitors, and we rarely had any trouble. In Nairobi we put up with the invasion for a few days, then had to send poor Ping to kennels. Dogs of all shapes came round. They fought outside our window, they made messes on the porch, they ruined the flowerbeds. One of them came from next door and I had to write and ask the people to keep the dog in at night because he was such a pest. Now I know there is the other side to this problem. I had a long talk to a lady in a queue for tickets for *Born Free* one day. She said she lived on a large farm and couldn't fence her dogs in, and she was sick of paying the vet to sew up her Ridgeback when he came back from fighting over a bitch.

'People who keep bitches ought to send them to kennels when they come in season,' she told me. I said I thought people who had dogs ought to make *some* effort to control them, and anyhow, if they kept bitches instead of dogs, it would be much simpler. I have always had a preference for bitches. The inconvenience of being in season is for me outweighed by the pleasure of pups, and I have no relish for the average dog and his leg-cocking everywhere, and the faithless way he will go off when there is an interesting bitch around. I was very sorry for poor Ping, who although well cared for at Kenya Kennels, hated it and didn't eat well. We decided to have her spayed. After all she was seven and had had four litters, amounting to a total of 18 puppies. All the same, when I took her up to the Small Animal Clinic at Kabete and handed her over, I felt a real Judas. She got over it very quickly, and I was able to collect her two days later. This was my first introduction to the team of vets who were later, two of them, to save Skipper's life. It was wonderful to feel you could really trust your dog to someone who actually seemed to *like* animals. I had been to many vets in India, Pakistan and Ceylon, and most of them seemed scared of dogs and not very knowledgeable, once you saw through the big talk and promises.

Mr Twohey, who ran Kenya Kennels so efficiently (and still does, I'm happy to say), warned me that Ping would have to be watched or she would grow fat. How right he was! She had always had a tendency to be too thin before, but now I gradually noticed a little corpulence about her, and ever since I have had to watch her diet. She has the pi-dog tendency to eat anything she can pick up and is a skilful beggar, sitting beside her victim with melting brown eyes, her ears going up and down as mouthfuls are swallowed. Occasionally, when the agony is just too much, she will wave an elegant white paw as a reminder. I hate a fat dog, and especially in a hot climate, as it is bad for the heart. I must say it was a relief not to have any more times when she was in season.

The barking dog menace loomed very large in our lives for several months at one time. As I have said, the garden sloped down to the stream, which ran through a valley at the bottom. The houses across the valley opposite us were mostly screened from us by trees, but the sound of a barking dog in one of the gardens could be very clearly heard, with the hillside throwing the sound across to us. It began very early one morning when my brother was staying with us. I was woken by persistent barking as if the dog was in trouble, so I got up with a torch and went out to investigate. I finally pinpointed the animal, a crossbred alsatian bitch, and she was not in a trap, as I'd feared. She was just standing in her garden and *barking* – just for the hell of it, I suppose. My appearance only had the effect of making her bark more, so I went back to bed but didn't sleep. Breakfast was a very angry meal. Chris had also been kept awake and we were all simmering. I walked over the stream carefully at a narrow point, and up the hill to the back door of the house, where I met the cook. I asked if anyone was in but was told no, Bwana was at work and Memsahib was out . . . I asked for the phone number and was given it, and later I drove round to look at the name board. (All houses in Ceylon and Kenya have their nameboard outside. I think it's a sensible idea we could copy in England). I then rang the gentleman at his office, not realising at that stage that it was in fact an Embassy; I'm dying to say which one, but I'd better not in case of diplomatic repercussions. I told him his dog had kept us awake and would he please keep it quiet, or better still, keep it in at night. He seemed to think I was a bit mad and gave the impression it was all good for a giggle, and I rang off not very hopeful of the future.

Sure enough, not many nights later we were kept awake again, until in despair we decided to hit back! I looked up the phone number in the book, and at 3 a.m. we rang the owner. When he at last answered (and he sounded very dozy), Leslie said 'Your dog is barking and keeping us awake, will you please keep it quiet,' and rang off before there was time for an answer. Not long after the barking stopped – for that night at least. Now at last we had a weapon, but it proved useless over Christmas and the New Year, when the family went away for ten days and left the dog with the servants . . . She barked and barked. I went over and told the servants to keep her quiet, but they said she was guarding and wouldn't help. Every morning and evening I would ring the house to see if they were back, and at last I got the wife. I wiped the floor with her and I must say, she sounded very apologetic in her broken English. Things were a little better after that, but I had heard that the local City Council was able to warn, and later prosecute, people whose dogs caused a nuisance, so I wrote to them and an inspector called round and warned the owner. In case you feel we were making a fuss about nothing, I must tell you that it is the most refined torture I know to lie in bed and listen to a big dog barking aimlessly, but with frightful regularity. She usually barked in fives, then a pause. Then another five and a pause. If the pause was long, you might begin to think she'd given up, but just as you were sinking into sleep, off she'd go again. I tried putting cottonwool in my ears but it was no help. Other people had the same trouble. There were often letters to the papers and we all had one insoluble problem: why weren't the owners woken up as well??? In our case, the dog was outside a bedroom window most of the time; it was incredible that they didn't hear it.

Anyhow, we went on leave and when we came back, what had been a mild skirmish had turned to out-and-out war. Not long after our return, we were woken up again and Leslie went to phone at some ungodly hour.

'Is that Mr A—?' he demanded.

'No,' replied a sleepy voice with a thick accent. 'He has gone away.'

'Well, your dog is keeping us awake, please keep it quiet or I will complain to the police,' snapped Leslie and hung up hastily.

Next day we had a council of war. We went and saw that there was indeed a new name up, so I decided to ring him and explain nicely and ask him please to keep the dog quiet.

Well, that must rank as one of the most infuriating and frustrating phone conversations of my career. I asked the 'gentleman' if he had taken over Mr A's dog and got no further. 'Who are you, what is your name?' he kept asking over and over again. 'Pierson,' I said, 'but I want —.' 'What is the name, Kerson? What is the name?' he demanded, 'You woke up my children in the night. You can go to hell.'

And he hung up on me . . .

That really did it . . . I went roaring off to the City Council and put in a report, and they promised to visit him and warn him. By this time I had found out that the enemy was something to do with an embassy, so I kept this bit of knowledge to myself, thinking that if the C.C. knew, they might not be able to act.

Days passed with no improvement. Sometimes we would have a quiet night, sometimes not. She would give a woof, and if it was early, we'd look at each other and hope she'd get it over with straight away. Your heart would give an awful lurch when she started up and when it was my turn to phone, it thumped like a dynamo.

We were very fair about phoning. We always waited at least at twenty minutes, and there was never any question, as the first owner had blithely suggested, that there were lots of other dogs who barked. Out of the twelve other dogs I knew who lived round us, all were kept in at night bar two and they seldom uttered . . .

One night Leslie rang. The enemy picked up the phone and immediately let off a burst of invective ending with 'son-of-a-bitch' and hung up. We were fit to be tied, though Leslie thought it was rather funny. What amazed us was that it was only 11 o'clock and for all he knew, we might have been his ambassador with an important message! Half an hour later the dog was still hard at it, so, still quivering, we rang again, both huddled over the phone to hear what he would say. He picked up the phone and without preamble said, 'If you do this again I will report you to the Director of Prosecutions,' and hung up. This set me off again, and I even went to the Police Station up the road. After our first call to him, he had told the patrol policeman, who visited the house each day to check, that someone called Kerson had been ringing him and disturbing him. The policeman came round to me next day and asked me if it was me. I told him it was and that Mr Whosis could expect a lot more nocturnal calls if he didn't keep his dog quiet. My object in going to the police was to get my story in first and to ask if I was in fact breaking the law in any way by my calls, as long as we weren't rude. They were very helpful, considering barking dogs are not their business, and said they thought it was the only way we could get our own back. Even so, I hated the whole stupid business. I like to have pleasant neighbours, and when we found out that the enemy was First Secretary, we realised why L. had had no answer to two letters sent to the Ambassador. We were appalled that a member of the Diplomatic Corps could behave so badly, and when the C.C. finally told us he had diplomatic immunity, it was not an unexpected irony. We were bitter enough at the shiny Mercedes with C.D. (Corps Diplomatique) plates that seemed to be allowed to do what they liked about town, and we felt a lot of the diplomats had a cushy life, all on the poor taxpayer. However, the C.C. advised me to write to the Minister of Protocol in Nairobi, which I did, and also spoke to him on the phone. He assured me that diplomats weren't allowed to do exactly as they pleased, and promised to do something, and actually things did improve. Then, to our relief, we left for a permanent posting here in Mombasa before the offending dog came into season. This was a time we dreaded, for unbelievable though it may seem, she was still sometimes left out in the garden in that state. The result was the most horrible dog-fights, and a litter of pups every six months. Once, I saw her with an Alsatian mating down by the stream and I rang Mrs A. She was a poor-sounding creature, very spineless (she always answered the phone at night. 'It is not our dog,' she would whine feebly, but it always shut up afterwards). I told her very clearly what was happening, and that in nine weeks' time there would be pups. Just to clarify the situation, I even suggested she ought to get the dog spayed or send her to kennels, but no one even bothered to come and collect the bitch and she soon had a second lover queueing up. Why on earth do such people keep a dog?

I have said we were not the only sufferers, and in fact the husband of a friend of mine used to be so incensed, he would drive round to the offending house and rattle the dustbin lid, raising cain, and when the startled owners emerged, he said he didn't see why they should sleep if he couldn't because of their bloody dog . . . I also heard of someone who poisoned some surrounding dogs who sent him mad. I hope it wasn't true, but I do understand how he felt.

The myth that the dog must be outside to guard is one that is well supported out here. A friend of mine kept an alsatian at night chained on each porch and one weekend they went away, leaving one dog on guard and two servant girls sleeping in the house. Thieves beat up the dog with a panga (a big flat bladed knife) and tried to disembowel her with a stick up her rectum . . . They then broke a window, put in a toto, who opened the door, and they quietly took what they wanted. The dog did in fact survive, but if she had been inside the house, as she now is, any toto coming through the window would have had a very warm reception!

Nowadays we live on top of a cliff by the sea, and sometimes the faint bark of a dog drifts over our two-acre plot and we say, 'Listen, a dog barking!' and we exchange a grin. The noise of the surf, the wind and the birds is about all we hear these days, and how we appreciate it. It's funny to look back on now, but it wasn't at the time and I managed to find five other people besides ourselves who were being kept awake; I never did persuade them to phone the enemy, the cowards!

CHAPTER 16

The Agricultural Show
and the Safari Rally

ONE ASPECT OF BEING POSTED to a small branch in Kenya was that I had to start from scratch in getting to know people and make friends. I had one contact, however, an Old Girl from my school, who, though not a contemporary of mine (she left the term before I arrived), sounded very hopeful. 'Elizabeth Morgan (now Carles)' I read in our O.G. Magazine news, 'is now settled happily in Kenya. She won several prizes for her ducks and horses in a local show.' This was the rough gist. Anyhow I lost no time in writing to Elizabeth before we arrived, and later, when we had settled in, I rang her. She immediately asked me round to coffee and I spent a happy morning being shown her livestock. She is indeed a kindred spirit, and has horses, dogs, cats, rabbits, goats, bantams and fowls. She also runs a flourishing riding school, and I immediately enrolled Sarah and Tessa. Sarah had done a little riding on leave and could trot, but under Elizabeth's brilliant tuition she blossomed into a really competent rider, which pleased me no end. Elizabeth was a strict but fair teacher, the children loved her, and she kept her ponies immaculate. I was able to take up riding again, to my great joy, and we had many wonderful hacks through the coffee estates around Kabete, down the wide grassy aisles that separated the fields. Through Elizabeth I met her next-door-neighbour-but-one, Betty Murray-Wilson, who was a fanatic Arab enthusiast. She had a pair of mares, mother and daughter, both pure Arabs, and we had many hectic rides on the pair of them. I used to ride the mother, Neddicke, who had a will of her own, and though not exactly iron-mouthed, I did find it took all my strength to stop her after a gallop sometimes.

Betty was keen to start an Arab stud and soon acquired a very pretty colt she named El Kheir; he was strawberry roan when he was a baby, but now he is much whiter. He has sired several foals and won a cup in the Arab class last year in the Nairobi Show. I had heard from Elizabeth

144

about this show, the biggest of the year in Kenya, with a large show ground with permanent stands and ring at Jamhuri Park on the outskirts of Nairobi. Elizabeth was busy preparing her animals to compete, for the show is for everything, rabbits, sheep, cows, goats, horses, poultry, eggs, butter, machinery – in fact, a real agricultural show. I offered to help her with her poultry, with memories of getting my own ready for our little Pet Show back in 1941. She jumped at my offer and I spent a happy morning scrubbing feet, cleaning beaks and burnishing combs. She had mostly Australorps, which are huge black birds. They normally have a placid nature, but they didn't relish our attentions. Believe me, it's quite a job delicately to prise out the dried mash that gets stuck inside the birds' nostrils! Anyway, at last we finished and the birds were put into the back of Elizabeth's long-suffering old Peugeot. She took out the back seat, put in a lot of straw, and with one or two of the more quarrelsome cocks stowed in cardboard boxes on the front seat, the remainder were left loose in the car with an African armed with a small stick sitting among them to keep the peace. It was quite a sight!

The Nairobi Show lasts five days, and apart from the stalls and trade stands, there is always something going on in the main arena. (Pigs, sheep and cattle had their own smaller rings.) There was the usual show jumping, parades by the armed forces, track-laying by the E.A. Railways and Harbours, log-cutting competitions, grand parade of livestock, and twice, in the evening after dark, a floodlit tattoo. This was superb, especially the massed bands, over 200 men and women, who marched and countermarched very smartly indeed. I adore this sort of thing in any country, and Kenya can hold its own anywhere in this sphere. There was also polo (somewhat hectic; I think the players were well tanked up beforehand!) and drilling, silently and in the dark, with a purple light showing up the white parts on the RAF uniforms. Police dogs demonstrated their skill, native dancers danced and drummed – it was a wonderful evening. We had been warned that it would be cold, and took cushions and a blanket. I was wearing two sweaters but even so, we were still only just comfortable.

The Show was responsible for a very anxious evening we spent waiting for Sarah to come home one night. She had an African friend whose father was an Inspector at our police station. Sarah came home one day from school, on the first day of the Show, and said that

Godensia had asked her to go with her to the tattoo. I really wasn't terribly keen, as I knew the tattoo wasn't on until Wednesday night, and I assumed they would merely be walking round the trade stalls. Anyhow, Sarah was so keen, I drove her up to the police station and met her father. He indicated a police van crammed full of Africans, men women and children, and said, when I asked, that they would be back 'about nine'. Glowing, Sarah and Godensia struggled into the van and drove off, waving gaily.

Nine o'clock came and no Sarah. When ten o'clock came, I rang the police station and asked where the van was. The Inspector on duty, another one whom I didn't know, said they wanted to know too, as some of his askaris were asking where their families were. He rang me back to say it was still at the show but leaving *now*. At eleven o'clock we rang again, this time to the police post in Jamhuri Park. Yes, it was leaving *now*, we were told. Finally, it turned up at 11.40. Sarah had had a marvellous time but had been cold. She was in a thin dress and cardigan and it had rained. She'd had no time for tea before she left and had had nothing to eat there. She gaily sat down to cottage pie and told us how super it had all been. It turned out that it had been a dress rehearsal of the Tattoo. I hadn't thought of that. Yes, she had been a bit cold, she admitted, but it was super fun . . .

The final excitement of the Show came when we heard that the huge Australorp rooster Elizabeth and I had so carefully prepared had won not only the Best Heavy Breed, but also The Best in Show! He had his picture in the paper, with Elizabeth in her white coat holding him, and she also won quite a lot with her other poultry and eggs. Her horses did well too, and Sarah had the experience of taking Chez Nous in the Arab Class, where Betty had also entered Heideh and Neddicke. Elizabeth had coached Sarah meticulously about how to lead Chez Nous and how to make her stand correctly, and she did very well and was in the final six. We then had to rush Chez Nous off and plait her mane to turn her into a child's pony for another class; we had forty minutes, but plaiting can be a very niggly job, and three of us were hard at it to get her ready in time.

We watched in awe as Elizabeth pranced forth on Sanderling for the side-saddle class. They looked marvellous, Elizabeth in black bowler and navy blue habit, Sanderling plaited and shining, hooves oiled and tack spotless. The previous year the show had taken place after we had moved down here, and I used eagerly to scan the paper each day to see how my friends had done. There was Elizabeth, side-saddle on Sanderling, the winner! Betty won with Kheir, and so everyone was happy, but I did feel out of it. We have a very good show here in Mombasa, that we went to last year, but it is not quite the same and is too far for people from Nairobi to bring stock to.

The end of the Show found us exhausted. We had been there on at least three days, and the last was so crowded it was frightening. I almost lost Tessa, squeezed behind me in the entrance gate, and my feet almost dropped off but it was worth it, and the organisers were highly praised and deservedly so. Even afterwards you felt you hadn't seen everything. I can never forget the Boran bulls. The Boran is a local breed for beef, the result of using the zebu, an Indian humped kind, to improve indigenous stock. The bulls are imposing, with huge humps and flapping dewlaps that almost touch the ground. They are good-tempered, and one breeder told me the cows with calves were the most fierce. She said a child could ride the bull she had. Most Borans are white or grey, with black points, so the rich brown Sahiwal was a nice contrast. These are usually hornless and have the large dewlaps, and, I think, the hump, but I may be wrong there. Anyhow, they are kindly and placid, and mingle good-naturedly with the more orthodox Jerseys, Herefords, Friesians and Angus. The Grand Parade was quite a sight, with the huge weaving line of cattle zigzagging round the arena. I felt sorry for the Merino sheep with their heavy fleeces, but they seemed to survive. It was a very English scene in many ways, but lately the African farmers are taking part. I saw a lovely photo in the paper of a Masai warrior leading his best bull round the ring at a local show; it looked most picturesque. At each show the African entries are going up, which is very heartening.

Another local event we always take a great interest in is the E.A. Safari Rally. This crazy event takes place every Easter weekend, when about ninety cars from all over the world go roaring off to cover 3,000 miles over some of the worst 'roads' in the world. They have a certain laid-down average speed to maintain between each checkpoint, and there is a limit as to how much of the car can be rebuilt in the process. Top drivers come from all over the world, but so far it has always been a local driver who has won. The route used to cover Kenya, Uganda and Tanzania, but this year, a month or two before the start, Tanzania suddenly informed the Safari Committee that either the rally started from Kampala or they would not allow the route to pass through Tanzania. The start has always been from Nairobi, as Kenya had the idea for the first rally back in 1953 for the Coronation. The Committee replied that it was too late to change the venue now, so Tanzania withdrew in a huff, tossing her head and saying 'Anyhow, it didn't do a country any material good to have lots of strangers tearing about advertising what rotten roads you had . . .'

Everyone gets very excited as the start looms closer; crowds gather by the Town Hall, and Mr Kenyatta always waves off the first car. He obviously enjoys himself hugely and stays for a long time, waving off a car every three minutes. Crowds line the route to wave and cheer, and in fact the poor drivers have trouble in getting out of the city because of crawling cars and crowds in the road.

Our favourite driver was Vic Preston because we always went to his garage in Nairobi. He has won the Safari and is always a popular competitor. Last year he showed his car to Neal and me and we were fascinated at the gadgets it had. Tip-back seats for the co-driver, back seat taken out to make room for spare wheels, thermos flasks, tools, equipment etc. Handles are put on the boot to help in pulling it out of mud, footplates are fitted to the back to stand on to bounce it out of soft ground, extra headlamps and a spotlight are fitted and a special meter to tell you what your average speed is and if you are keeping to it.

How many finish depends a lot on whether it's been wet or dry. Last year it was so wet that only seven finished out of over 90. This year it was dusty, which most drivers hate more than rain. The huge billowing clouds of red dust can stop a car from passing a slower one and hold him back unless the leader is sporting enough to wave him on. Last year everyone was thrilled when two ladies managed to finish the course under the most appalling conditions. They said the worst part was finding somewhere private to spend a penny!

Everyone glues themselves to the radio and television for three days, petrol stations put up a blackboard with latest scores, for a driver who is late to check in is given penalty points. These are also given for various repairs that may be made. After the race, all the finishers are rigorously scrutineered, that is the car is taken to bits to see that there has been no funny business. Parts that must not be replaced have been marked with special paint, and these are checked to see they are still intact.

Things have changed a lot since the first Safari Rally in 1953, and with the participation of teams put in by manufacturers, competition is almost too keen and feelings run high. The Safari this year was marred by an objection to the winners when everyone, including the Mayor of Nairobi, was assembled to watch the trophies presented. The winning pair, Hillyard and Aird, had already had a tough time after the scrutineers had found some sort of valve (I think it was) that was very slightly larger than the usual one for that type of car. The makers in Germany had to be contacted to confirm that this was not an isolated alteration for just that car, but one that had been incorporated into many other similar cars, but of which the Safari scrutineers had had no notification. In the end they managed to produce the evidence just in time and thought they were all right, when the objection was lodged. The Press reported lost tempers and angry scenes, but in the end it was all sorted out. The objectors were told that if they stuck to their guns, the case would have to be referred to the U.K. for arbitration and the result of the Safari would be held up for weeks. This caused them to withdraw the objection and at long last proceedings were allowed to continue.

Mostly, the sportsmanship in the Safari seems to be pretty good, as far as an onlooker can see, but each time one hears the odd report of someone sulking over a judge's decision or a rule. However, this seems common in most sports. Our friend Vic Preston gave a fine exhibition of good sportsmanship last year, when he and Bob Gerrish failed to get their card stamped at a certain checkpoint and were disqualified from the rally. They appealed but once it was turned down, they accepted it. They were highly experienced drivers and no exception could be made for them. This year the same thing happened but the driver, another experienced rallyist, was very petulant over the incident and the makers of his car said huffily that they might not enter next year, which sounded really ludicrous, coming from grown men.

A legitimate grievance that many drivers did have, however, was the amount of stone-throwing in rural areas. In 1968, one driver was hit by a rock hurtling through his windscreen when he was doing over 60 m.p.h., and he was forced to retire and have several stitches put in. No one seems quite sure of the reason for this dangerous practice: whether some of the local inhabitants object to vast cars hurtling through their village, probably killing a few hens and menacing any stray children, or whether it is children doing it for a joke. This year most of the incidents were in Uganda, after some very strong warnings from the top that such behaviour would be punished. It is well nigh impossible for the police to catch the culprits, for most of the rally is over mere tracks, right out in the bush. Another hazard faced by drivers is animals crossing the road, and one driver who was leading in 1968 had victory snatched from him near home when a buck ran across his path and caused him to hit a bank and retire.

Just after this year's Safari, it was announced that the 1970 Rally would start from Dar es Salaam in Uganda. We all hope that arrangements will go off satisfactorily there. Few people realise the fantastic work and organisation involved in the Rally, which is continuous, plans for the next going ahead as soon as the last is over.

CHAPTER 17

Safaris to Naivasha and Amboseli

THE SAFARI HAS A marked effect on driving in Nairobi over Easter.
Coming back from seeing the start out on the Mombasa Road,
one battles through would-be enthusiasts in Fiats, which isn't too bad,
but when it is Mercedes, it is a different matter, as they tear past, horn
blaring. It used to be the same coming back from Nakuru, where we
sometimes used to go to watch the car racing. It is a very pleasant
track, where spectators sit on a hillside overlooking the circuit, this
being visible all the time. Nakuru also has a large soda lake which is
the home of thousands of flamingos. As you approach the town, you
catch a glimpse of the lake in the distance and the pink ring of birds
round the edge is like a necklace. It is a pleasant place for a picnic and
can be reached in a two-hour drive from Nairobi.

Another good spot for bird watchers is Lake Naivasha, only an
hour's drive on the Nakuru Road. The lake teems with birds of all
kinds: coots, herons, fish eagles, kingfishers, ducks, egrets and many
more. I believe over 200 species are to be found either on the water or
beside it among the papyrus and weed at the edge. The place is,
however, being increasingly marred by speed boats, which reminds me
of a boat trip we took Mummy on when she came to stay with us in
Nairobi. We decided she must see Naivasha, so we ordered a boat by
phone and turned up one fine morning to see the sights. The start was
slightly marred by the children taking cushions from the boathouse,
which we subsequently found out cost 1/- each to hire. 'It'll be more
than the cost of the boat at this rate,' muttered Leslie as he cast off. We
chugged off gamely but soon came to a halt when we discovered we
had fouled some cunningly concealed fishing nets. I hung perilously
over the stern, sawing away at the tough nylon strands that were so
tightly wrapped around the propeller. At last, muttering darkly, we
were free and puttered off once more. Not long after, a speed boat
came into view behind us as we were entering a narrow channel cut
through heavy weed and half submerged trees. It was temporarily

forced to slow down to our dignified put-putting but as soon as we emerged into a wider channel, it swept past us at full throttle and surged off, leaving us with two inches of freeboard and some frightened children. The adults were fit to be tied. We were seething with rage but we didn't know the name of the boat and only knew that the culprits were a nasty-looking middle-aged couple. Consequently we could do nothing but hope they sank in the next storm that blew up.

We once stayed for a few days at a hotel on the edge of the lake. It was memorable only for its expense and for the fact that the menu for lunch on day one was:

Brown Windsor soup (Yes, honestly, I swear!)

Cottage Pie.

Rice pudding.

The fact that it was very *nice* cottage pie hardly helped the seaside boarding house atmosphere engendered by this menu. The nicest thing about our stay was the hippo who lived near the water's edge. When we took my brother to the lake on a visit, we saw her actually come out of the water and Chris has an excellent movie film of her with a herd of cows. One cow, not liking the intruder, lowered its head and charged rather half-heartedly, and the hippo retreated. Unfortunately the cowherd waved his arms and threw sticks at the hippo, who later retired moodily back to the water. She seems to be a loner, as I have never seen any other hippos in the lake.

While Chris was staying with us, we took him to Amboseli, which we had heard and read was great rhino country. It was a very good holiday indeed; we lived in three little thatched bandas, which looked straight out on to Mount Kilimanjaro. Most of the time the summit was buried under cloud but occasionally one had a glimpse of the dazzling snow through the veil.

We had been told that Ol Tukai Old Lodge was a do-it-yourself camp, so we were loaded with food, pots and pans and bedding. A nice old man appeared, however, and adopted us, showing us round and making the beds up. Each banda had a little open veranda at the front, with a table and chairs on it, and a big bedroom with two iron beds, which boasted Dunlopillo mattresses. There was also a bathroom with a proper loo, so we weren't 'roughing it' too badly. Then our guide led us to a smaller hut behind our banda and flung open the door. There, squatting malevolently in a corner, was an evil-looking black Dover Stove. Embossed across the oven door was its name, 'The Caledonian Combat'.

I'm sure our guide thought we were quite mad as we burst into hysterical laughter and were forced to support ourselves against the doorpost. Luckily he knew exactly how to handle the monster and after feeding it with wood and blowing judiciously, soon had a good heat going to cook the lunch.

That night about nine o'clock we heard lions roaring and an elephant screaming as though there was a fight going on. It was the most exciting noise I have ever heard and we were thrilled. I had seen elephant droppings near our banda and paced the distance from them to us. It was 23 paces! In the night I was woken up by strange thudding hooves outside and an odd barking noise. Immensely intrigued, I crammed on a sweater over my pyjamas and went out on to the veranda to investigate.

There was half a moon, so it was fairly light, and after a moment my eyes got more used to the change. Milling about a short distance away from me was a large herd of zebra. They seemed to be in a panic and completely disorganised as they galloped past, their eyes glowing red in the beam of my torch. Entranced, I sat down to watch and listen. Finally, the zebra departed, so I went back to bed. After a few minutes I heard another noise and up I got again. This time, it was the blowing and splashing of elephants at a nearby waterhole. Greatly daring, I walked cautiously out to the low line of stone that marked the camp boundary ('Do not go beyond this point' admonished a large notice, and I didn't). I stood on the stones and shone my torch in the direction of the noise, ready to flee back to my banda if necessary. Then I picked up the glowing red eye of an elephant. I didn't dare stay too long but went back to my chair. The moon shone on the snow on top of Kilimanjaro, and there was no noise except natural ones – no planes or car engines, no voices, only exciting snorts and splashes and the trill of crickets. I forced myself back to bed again, but in all I got up four times and sat for over an hour. Chris had also been woken up and joined me for a bit. It was an unforgettable experience, which is a very trite phrase to use but nevertheless apt.

One of the great attractions about Ol Tukai was the vast numbers of very tame birds that abounded. The most spectacular was the Superb

Starling, well-named, with its glossy purplish-green body, black head and orange breast. It had a fierce white eye with a black pupil that glared at you and demanded food. Mingled with these were some golden weavers, the males like exaggerated canaries, with brilliant orange heads and yellow bodies, the females duller and browny-grey. They descended on us as soon as we sat down to lunch on the first day and we threw them titbits. Some even had the sauce to come on to the table and chairs, but it was only after patient waiting that I finally persuaded a starling to feed from my hand. We paid a visit to Ol Tukai New Lodge, a few hundred yards away, for a pre-lunch drink, and sat out on a patio that was lined with feeding tables. Clouds of weavers nested in nearby trees, and also flew into the dining room for food. It was like an exotic kind of Trafalgar Square, they were so thick under foot. Also around our bandas were smart pink and black hoopoes, with long curved beaks that probed the ground as they pattered busily along in search of grubs. One couple had a large baby that was a perfect pest and followed them about begging infuriatingly, but was quite capable, when left to himself, of finding his own food.

We went out twice a day with a ranger to look for game and were very disappointed to see no rhino at all. We drove over the weird-looking dried-up lake and saw the mirage ahead of water and trees. It was very eerie. White dust swirled all over it, and you expected to find bleached bones lying about everywhere. In the distance a herd of scrawny cattle was being driven across the waste by some Masai herdsman. Books about Africa are so popular these days, and the Masai so well known, that I don't intend to repeat a description of this fine people and their ways. Ironically, in an age when most African governments decry the colonial imperialist and his wicked ways, the Tanzanian government recently launched a campaign to modernize the Masai. They said his habit of wearing only a blanket that tended to expose his buttocks must be curbed. He must wear trousers and he must not smear his face with red ochre nor even pierce his ears. Visitors to the country must not get the impression that the Masai were savages, so they must be brought up to date. As a crowning insult, he has been removed from the currency notes! The Masai has been one of the few tribes who actually resist outside pressures of civilisation. The Masai herdsman lives only for his cattle. For any country to try to change these fine looking warriors is a crime, but

*Tess keeps a safe distance while Sarah pats Rufus the rhino,
an orphan at Tsavo, 1966.*

children in Tanzania have actually been told by the government to jeer
and mock at any Masai they see in traditional dress. Thank goodness
those who live in Kenya are free to dress how they please. We in Kenya
are also free to wear mini-skirts, which some of our neighbours have
outlawed, even employing special guards of 'trained' young men to
enforce the order (Tanzania again; one can't help feeling the nicest
thing about that country today is Mount Kilimanjaro).

It was strange that we saw no rhino at Amboseli, but even odder that
one should cross the Mombasa road when we were taking Chris on a
visit to the coast after Amboseli. I have never seen one since and we
watch Chris's movie of it with great glee each time we go on leave. It
came out beautifully, ambling across the tarmac, then trotting off into
the bush with its tail in the air.

We were lucky to meet a famous rhino in Tsavo Game Park. He had
been reared as a tiny baby by the Sheldricks. Denis was a Game
Warden there and kept several orphan elephants, rhino and buffalo.
They all wandered free, supervised by a guard, and we gave Rufus
some oranges, which he chomped up eagerly. For his size – and he was
almost fully grown – he had an odd voice, just like a small calf's, a

pathetic mooing sound. He was very well-known and always had lots of visitors. Daphne Sheldrick was in a lovely film about the Tsavo orphans, which we saw on TV many years later. Eleanor the Elephant and Buster the Buffalo had been only half-grown when we saw them, but Eleanor became the foster mother to all new baby elephants. We felt really privileged to feel we'd met them in the flesh.

CHAPTER 18

A win for Skip and illness

ALL TOO SOON TWO YEARS had passed and we were due to go on our three months' leave again. For the first time we found we were not as keen as usual. Nairobi life was in many ways similar to the U.K.; there was plenty in the shops, in fact all the advantages of climate and comfortable living. Also, I wasn't looking forward to our first leave since Poppa had died. Mummy was still living in the little Oxted flat and seemed happy there, but there would be a big gap without him. Mother's circumstances were also changed; she was due to move from the hospital to the big house Bill had bought at Ayot.

The Hollands arrived to take over business and pets and we were glad to leave the dogs in such good hands. I was sorry we were going to miss the Shaggy Dog Show in July, but I gave Margaret strict instructions to attend and told her exactly how to wash and prettify the dogs for the big event. she promised she would enter them and would let me know the results.

Poor Ann and Mummy had a frightful time finding a house for us to live in. We had a spate of letters: Yes, they had a possible one. No, sorry, it had fallen through, but another had been found. Oh, the owners had changed their minds. Don't worry, we'll find something, and in the end they did. 'Freshfields' proved to he a misnomer if ever there was one, but it was in a lovely part of Surrey at South Godstone, only ten minutes' drive from Mummy and forty minutes from Ann. The owner lived abroad and the house had been empty for months, so Ann warned us on the way that the garden was a wilderness. How right she was! The lawn was three feet high and it was hard to tell which was flower bed. Roses fought their way up gamely through the brambles, but smaller flowers just gave up trying. Inside the house we found some interesting bullet holes in Neal's window (they were the real thing, all starry; evidently they were the work of some yobs passing when the house was empty). The dining room chairs appeared to have been used for draining fish and chips. They were *black* with grease.

Stan Holland took this of Ping at the Shaggy Dog Show,
Nairobi, 1967. It was the year that Skip won the Shaggiest Dog class.

Anyhow we settled in happily, and it was nice not to have to worry too much about keeping the place spotless.

The day of the Shaggy Dog Show arrived and I wondered how things had gone. I had reckoned that if Margaret wrote at once we might hear by Wednesday, but on Monday morning, before breakfast, the postman arrived with the mail and a telegram!

'Skipper unplaced Veterans won Shaggy Dog, Cup, Rosette and all. Newspaper cuttings, photos, follow.'

You can imagine how we felt . . . Clever little dog! Marvellous Margaret, she must have really made her look super. Breathlessly we waited for the photos, which arrived a few days later. 'Skipper Leads the Field' said a headline over a picture of Skip, Lesley and the cup. The latter was *vast*, with a huge rosette, red, green and blue, attached to it. There were reports in two papers plus three press glossy prints. It was most exciting. The ironic thing about it all was that the class I was so

Cup and rosette for Best in Show, Nairobi Shaggy Dog Show, 1967.

keen for Skipper to be entered for was the Veteran. I hadn't even considered the Shaggy Dog Class. I knew it came right at the end of the show, and last time we left before it as I thought there were bound to be hairier dogs than Skip. Anyhow, when we later met Margaret and got the full story, she told us she had been determined to stick it out to the bitter end. 'I promised Jenny I'd put her in, and I will,' she told an embittered Stan, who soon tired of sitting on hard seats watching endless processions of odd-looking dogs and doting owners. At long last, after prolonged agony as several new classes had been put in before the big moment, in they went, Lesley and Skip. I gather one of the judges was Mr Slade, the Speaker of the House, who had a very old dog himself; I don't know if she was in the class. Anyhow, to the vast surprise and delight of the weary Holland family, the big silver cup, donated to the S.P.C.A. each year by a betting firm, was presented to Skip, who then had to pose for photographers. I shall always regret we were not there to see the fun!

Towards the end of our leave, Margaret had to come home to put Lesley in to school, leaving Stan on his own for some weeks. Although he was willing to look after the dogs, we felt that it was too risky with him at the office most of the day and with the house being near the road with no gate. The dogs were therefore sent to Kenya Kennels, to Mr Twohey, who had had them several times before on short stays when we had gone away on safari. He was very kind and wrote twice during that month to tell us the dogs were well.

Our three months flew past as it always does, and we left U.K. in October. Stan and David met us at the airport and took us home. I immediately rang the kennels to say we were back and that we would be round right away to collect the dogs. Mrs Twohey answered the phone and after the preliminaries were over, she told me that 'little Skipper hasn't been at all well.' The way she said 'little' sent my heart plummeting as she went on to say she had something wrong with one eye and wouldn't eat. She was in a darkened room and the vet saw her every day . . . I promised to come at once and as Leslie wanted to unpack, Stan drove me. It was a foul wet day and I sat numbly beside Stan, watching the streaming windscreen and thinking the thoughts every dog-lover has when an old friend is ill.

We arrived at last and Mr Twohey carried out a grubby, woebegone looking object. Usually the dogs are beautifully bathed and brushed before they are handed back to their owners, but Skip was too ill for that and I was shocked at her appearance. Mr Twohey told us she ate almost nothing; he sat for ages every day, tempting her with bits of liver, chicken, Chappie – everything. He has about 200 dogs to cope with, so I was terribly grateful. He had tried so hard with her. 'I'm ashamed to give her back to you like this,' he said, 'she's just skin and bone.' She was too; every rib could be felt and she was very weak. He said the vet diagnosed an abscess in the eye and she was having ointment put into it. There was a bare patch round the eye where she had scratched it, and on the actual eyeball was a horrid little sort of pothole. While I was writing this, I had a look at the eye and the dent has gone, but I know it stayed for some months after her illness. I took her straight up to my own vet at Kabete for a second opinion and they said the same as the first vet and that we should continue with the ointment. From the time we got home, Skipper perked up. She ate well, to my amazement, and after a few days I rang Mr Twohey to tell him, for he had been extremely worried about her. He was so pleased, as he later told me, 'I was just praying she'd live long enough for you to take her back,' and we came to the conclusion that she missed having people around. Good as Mr Twohey is with his charges, he cannot keep them all in his home and companionship was obviously what she missed when she was ill; she always sits at my feet if I am at home and will come trailing after me even if I go to the bathroom. I hear a clattering of claws on the tiled floor and then a mighty 'fifff' under the door as she checks to see if I'm at home. Margaret says they both do the same when she first takes them over, literally dogging her footsteps. Within a month she was back to her old self. The hair grew on her bald patch and the fringe covered her bad eye.

Plans started to materialize for a move down to Mombasa. We had a visit from one of our London Directors and he told Leslie to start looking for a house there. Already two other tea companies had moved down so as to be on the spot for shipping their tea. Most tea sales take place near the port for this reason, and Nairobi auctions were the only ones that were 300 miles from the place of shipment. I viewed the move with a certain amount of gloom. I would miss my riding; no one seemed to know of any horses in Mombasa. It would break up the girls' schooling. They were well settled in at Hospital Hill School, in a very happy, multi-racial atmosphere. I would miss my old friends too, Betty and Elizabeth especially, and there was talk of the move in about July. Meanwhile I was dying for Skip to have another crack at the Shaggy Dog Show. Also, Mombasa has no television yet and I'm a great addict. Anyhow, on one or two holiday visits we looked at some houses, but they were mostly either too expensive or just plain unsuitable. We stayed twice in a house on Nyali Estate, a private residential area, in a nice bungalow overlooking the sea. Next door was an identical bungalow, owned also by Gailey and Roberts, and it transpired that G&R would be willing to sell it and buy our Nairobi house. On our last visit, over Easter 1967, the next door bungalow was empty, so knowing it might be our home, we got the key and swarmed over it. It is a pleasant one-storcy house, with a big veranda looking out over the garden and with the sea beyond. It is on a cliff about 40 feet high, so we are not bothered too much by spray, and usually catch a good breeze. We have a path down to the beach, which is beautiful, with white stretches of sand and palm trees waving in the breeze. The garden is on a two-acre plot, about half of which, at the back, is just grass dotted with trees and bushes, but it does ensure you're not cheek-by-jowl with your neighbour and I've already said how peaceful it is after Nairobi.

CHAPTER 19

Surgery for me, Skipper and the cat!

1968 STARTED VERY EVENTFULLY but in rather a nasty sort of way, with my paying a visit to hospital; I hate to be coy. It was for a piles operation and anyone who has suffered it will know what it entailed, so I won't dwell on it. I was in a ward, and I much prefer it to a private room. You can't feel too worried for yourself when you can see others who are just as bad, and once you get used to seeing unconscious victims of the scalpel coming and going, it is rather fun. Of course the lack of privacy is a slight drawback, but it gave me some giggles and I pulled through. Leslie came every afternoon, and I had a 'Get Well' card signed by all the office staff, plus flowers, which was most touching. Leslie was kept busy at home caring for the dogs and also our newest pet, a half-Siamese female cat we named Tigga. I had always hankered for a cat and Leslie mumbled that if we had a bloody cat, it had better be a proper Siamese . . . I answered an advertisement at the Cattery for a Siamese Tom and went to see him. I was told that he had been left at the house of some folk who had left Kenya. They had asked a friend to take their dog, and by chance she had found the cat too, abandoned. I just cannot understand such heartlessness. He was a beautiful cat, a full-blown tom, but his age and past history were unknown; he would have to be neutered, which would take time, and I had really wanted a kitten. The Cattery lady showed me an elegant half Siamese in a pen with her mother, who was pure Siamese; she was named Celeleh (which is Swahili for noise) and certainly had the usual piercing voice of her kind. Her daughter was three months old, demurely sitting, her tail curved round her. She had pale blue eyes, and where she ought to have been chocolate, she was tabby striped. Her body was the correct biscuity colour. I was very smitten but undecided, so rang L., who said he'd leave it to me and I chose her. She cost me twenty shillings and I cancelled my tentative order with the Cattery lady for an as-yet unborn Siamese, thereby saving some money. Tigga is always called 'That Twenty Shilling Cat' by Leslie when she has killed a bird or been sick on the carpet. We called her Tigga because she bounced such a lot, and also because of her stripes. She turned into a very aloof type, not a lap-sitter at all, as I'd planned, but she looks lovely. She got on well with the dogs. They were fascinated but cautious, and she spat at them a bit but later became special friends with Ping, whom she would chase, ambush and wrestle with till the rugs flew in all directions. They both adored it. Tigga would pretend to be livid, with her ears flat back, tail lashing, and Ping used to growl furiously as they rolled about the floor or chased down the passage. Skip could sometimes be persuaded to join in, but would growl jealously at her and slink off in an unsporting way. We did not let Tigga out at night and she slept in the hall on a cushion, with a sand box close by. She used to get lost quite often when she was small, and we would wander about calling futilely, since she only comes when she feels like it. Usually she would be found in the depths of a cupboard or drawer, fast asleep. She also had the habit of tearing up trees and then getting stuck. This was all right until one day, New Year's Day to be precise, she shot twenty feet up a eucalyptus tree by the boundary fence and there she stuck. We decided she needed a lesson, so we left her there for about three hours. After lunch we went out again to call her and she looked very unhappy. By this time she was getting sleepy and was liable to 'drop off' very literally indeed. As we stood there, a Norwegian professor who lived in a next-door flat came up to see what was going on. I explained and without further talk, he proceeded to remove his socks and shoes and began to shin up the tree. I stood at the bottom, petrified in case he should fall and knowing Tigga would not welcome his attentions. Sure enough, she clung to the branch grimly and when he prised her off, transferred her claws to her rescuer's shoulders. Unperturbed, he climbed down and handed her over to me, laughed off my incoherent thanks and departed. At least she had learnt her lesson and never again got stuck, although she often went quite high.

One night while I was in hospital, she led Leslie an awful dance. Skipper was suddenly sick and as he opened the veranda door to put her outside in disgust, Tigga slipped out into the garden. I thought it was very kind of Leslie, considering he is not a cat-lover, to trail her round the garden rattling her enamel dish and calling 'Tiggy, Tiggy, Tiggy' in that ridiculous falsetto we seem to use for cat-calling. She strung him along in true feline fashion, waiting till he was a few feet away, then hopping neatly away into another inaccessible spot. After an unfruitful ten or fifteen minutes of this hide-and-seek, Leslie told her she could bloody well STAY out then and stamped indoors and shut her out. She was found next day up a tree looking cold and reproachful. L. told me the story in the car as he was taking me home from hospital, and I almost had a relapse from laughing. 'It wasn't at all funny,' he said in dignified reproach. 'Blasted animal, it was the way she waited for me *almost* to catch her before moving.' I told him soothingly I was most impressed at his devotion to duty.

We had a date booked for the unsuspecting animal to be spayed, but in fact we ended up with two animals on the operating table, and I spent the worst few days I can remember as a result. It began with Skip getting cystitis. One evening she suddenly began to pass blood and scream with pain and strain. I rang the vet and took her up to Kabete, where a very pleasant African that I hadn't met before gave her a very thorough check-up. He thought it was cystitis and gave her an antibiotic injection and some sedative pills to help her sleep. He told me to bring her back next day, when Dr Sayer would be there. She had a good night and was improved next day. Dr Sayer confirmed the diagnosis and we kept up the pills. She was fine almost immediately. About a week later, however, I suddenly realised she seemed too lethargic and off her food. She lay all day in her basket but as it was raining a lot, I assumed she didn't want to get her feet wet and that was why she went out so little.

After two days I decided something must be wrong, so to test her I took her out in the park, a place she usually loves, running gaily along, investigating all the smells and greeting other dogs. I shall never forget her expression as I set her down on the path and said 'Come on, lovely walks.' She stood pathetically, tail drooping, and reluctantly walked a few steps to please me, but obviously something was very wrong. She refused to eat for two days too, so off we went to see Paul Sayer again. He examined her, and we noticed for the first time she had a discharge, pointing to some disorder of the uterus. He thought he knew what was wrong, but wanted me to leave her for more tests and X-rays. Dr Colgrove looked at her too. She had seen Skip before when I was having trouble with the little dog's gremlins. Really she seemed haunted. She would suddenly give a jump, peer wildly behind her, clamp her tail down and sit shivering and panting at my feet, just as she did during thunderstorms. This happened so often, I went to the vet, feeling very silly, because it is difficult to move about cooking supper with a small haunted dog permanently on your feet. We never did find the reason. We saw no insect that might have stung her, she had no fleas or ticks to worry her, and once I set her off by inadvertently dropping a tiny piece of flakey pastry on her; that was the only time we knew the reason for her terror. Anyhow, a very mild sedative pill helped, and after we came back off leave, she seemed to have left her tormentors at the kennels. Dr Sayer used to tease me about the gremlins; he had never had such a case before.

Now Skip was really ill and they told me that if their suspicions were correct, they would have to perform a total hysterectomy on her, as she had pyometra. I tried to weigh up the situation sensibly. Skip was now 13; this was her birthday month. She had been very fit but now I wondered if it was fair to expect her to go through the discomfort and pain of a major operation. I tried to put this to the sympathetic vets and they both assured me that the recovery rate was very high, and that they had done the op. on dogs even older than she with success. The trouble came from a hormone imbalance that caused a build-up of pus in the uterus, and the relief after removal of this was so great, they assured me she would be all right. They told me to leave her anyhow for further tests and as I was bringing up Tigga next day for her op., I could find out then about Skip.

My old friend stood on the metal table and it was a measure of how ill she was that she wasn't even shaking, as she usually does as soon as she get to the door. Dear kind Mrs Trendall, who is the receptionist there, took Skip from me and said: 'Try not to worry too much, but I know it's no good saying that, you will; we all do, don't we?' I was in tears by then and gave Skip a final(?) pat. Then I drove home very slowly and carefully, because I couldn't see too well.

Next day I took Tigga up, feeling a heel, and they said Skip's tests still indicated a pyometra (I think that is the term) and they would operate next day. Tigga was done that afternoon and she almost died; she got emphysema and they had a job to pull her through, not helped by the fact that they knew Skip would be next.

Next day, trying to keep terribly busy, I rang about four and was told Skip was still 'out' but that the operation had gone off well. They said

Tigga was feeling 'low' and that I could collect her now, as she needed tender home care. I was shocked at how miserable she looked, her fur standing up and her movements slow and painful. She wouldn't wash, eat or even purr for two days. Then suddenly she decided to start to live again and began to wash, eat and purr, to our relief. She used to sit and stare at me until I was sure she knew I was responsible for her discomfort. It was agony to watch her move for those first few days.

I didn't let myself hope Skip would survive, and had at least one session locked in the lavatory crying my eyes out. It is no use whatsoever on these occasions telling yourself, 'It's only a dog, why the fuss?' Leslie's attitude was that she had had a long life and if she died, she died. He hates emotional scenes.

She had the operation on Friday. On Saturday, when I had fetched Tigga, they had said she was walking about a bit and they hoped she'd eat. I told them she liked 'Chappie' and they said later she did in fact eat some. On Monday I rang and was told I could take her home. The clouds lifted and I sang as I drove up the Vet. Lab. Hill. I met Betty coming down and she said they had told her Skip was marvellous; I was so pleased.

An assistant carried her out to me. She looked a bit tangly and had seven black, practical-looking stitches down her tum, which they told me would have to come out in a week. Off we went and when I got her home, I found she wouldn't walk properly but hopped along on three legs, using the fourth, back one, to scratch frantically at the sutures. I was afraid she might pull them out, so I swaddled her round with a large elastic bandage, but she went about irritatingly on three legs for weeks after the stitches were out.

The two convalescents used to lie together in the armchair by me as I wrote letters, so I could keep an eye on them. Tigga was a model patient and never tried to interfere with her sutures. They looked sweet together. I was so happy now, so you can understand my feelings when two days later Skip suddenly began to pant, shiver and lie about not eating. My heart sank, I took her temperature, it was two degrees above normal. Finally, about 9 o'clock, I rang Dr Sayer and he told me to bring her up immediately. It may seem strange but a part of me gave up; I had had enough. 'If you're going to die, do it, and do it quickly. I cannot keep this up.' I felt guilty as we drove through the pelting rain, and I wondered what would happen if I had a puncture in such a lonely spot, for the Vet. Lab. is at the top of a hill out in the middle of nowhere. We got there safely and kind Dr Sayer was there, looking odd without his white coat, like a helmetless policeman. He took her temperature, gave her an injection and handed me some pills for her.

'Will she be all right?' I asked in a shaky voice,' because I can't take much more of this and if she's not going to get better, I'd rather she was put down now.' (How many times had I re-lived this scene in the past few days, handing her over for the last time to be put to sleep, lying in bed in the dark, wallowing in it?) Sayer assured me it was only a slight infection and how right he was. She never looked back after that. They told me she was 10lbs when she went in (she had been 11lbs when we came to Kenya) and that she weighed 9½lbs after the operation, so one can imagine the relief she had. They had also cleaned her teeth and removed three loose ones, so she looked fine. A few months later, before we moved down to Mombasa, we went to say goodbye to Dr Colgrove, (Dr Sayer had left by then) and we weighed her. She was over 12lbs, and Dr Colgrove said she was a small miracle and remarked how very rewarding these cases were to a vet. I shall never forget the kindness of the Kabete staff; they have given Skip borrowed time that we all appreciate.

There, that is the end of all the sad bits of this book. It has a happy ending, in case you are wondering, as I always do if I read a book about an animal. It's much nicer if it ends happily!

CHAPTER 20

The move to Mombasa
and the coming of Mousie

IT MAY SOUND EXTREMELY SILLY, but I had a deep antagonism towards the move to Mombasa for the simple reason that I thought we would miss the Shaggy Dog Show by a very narrow margin! The move had to be carefully planned in a week where there was no sale of tea in Nairobi. Leslie found a convenient week at the beginning of August and plans went ahead, with me muttering away in the background. I had seen a vague mention of the Shaggy Dog Show in the paper, and it had mentioned an August date. Nothing I or the children could say would persuade my husband that the move could wait a week. I was so keen for Skip to enter because of her operation and my pride in her survival. Some men have no sense of proportion at all, and he refused point blank to alter any arrangements. Glumly I looked at Skip, who had gone into a dreadful moult after the operation. Her tail especially was reduced to a humiliating rat-like appendage, and Dr Colgrove put her on hormones to try and encourage it to grow more hair. This succeeded and by March things were almost back to normal. Thoroughly discouraged, I trimmed her ears one day; the feather on them was so long and tangly. A few days later we saw a notice in the paper that the Show was to be held in the last Sunday of July, just a week before the move. The girls and I gave a cheer, but then I started wringing my hands over her ears. All I could do was to trim the edges neatly and hope they would grow a bit in the couple of months left to us.

My whole attitude to the move changed (stupid, isn't it?) and I started to take an interest in the plans. Packing up all our stuff would take a whole day, as we were taking nearly all the furniture with us. The journey, by road, would take us a morning, so we decided to pack (or be packed, rather, by professionals) all day Friday, sleep in a hotel on Friday night, and leave early next morning to be at the Nyali house to greet the moving van, which would leave the night before.

Arrangements had to be made to find jobs for the servants, neither of whom wanted to come with us so far away from their homes in Nairobi. Just before we left Nairobi, poor Henry Cuddles, our hamster that we had had for nearly three years, died. I felt terribly guilty over his death; he went off his feed and moped about, and when I called in Mr Lawson, the expert on these little animals, he immediately looked at poor Henry's teeth. To my horror, he showed me how the bottom front incisors had grown enormously and had even pierced the roof of his mouth, making it almost impossible for him to eat. Mr Lawson calmly snipped down the teeth with a pair of cutters and I was almost sick over his shoes . . . We were too late to save Henry; he was old and weak and he died shortly after. Mr Lawson said it was a common mishap, and that older hamsters had to be inspected and have their teeth trimmed at intervals. We decided to buy a replacement and went to Mr Lawson's to choose a new one. We were fascinated by his collection of hamsters of all ages and colours. He kept full records of all litters born, parents, etc. and it was all very professional. We finally chose a youngster called Paddy but we were very smitten with a golden one that had a white band round the tummy. Another kind had a white band with a pale, sandy body colour. We weren't sure which we liked best, but we ordered one of either colour as a mate for Paddy, and he promised to mate two for us so that we could take the baby before we went. Hamsters are efficient breeders (in some cases, though we had singular lack of success later). The female comes in season every five days, and the mating time is the only time hamsters meet, once they have been separated from their mother, for they are horribly quarrelsome and even a female will fight a male if she is not in season. We took Paddy home chittering with rage, and settled down to wait for the baby to be born. Mr Lawson said he always mated two females at the same time so that if there was any trouble, and a mother died, the other could foster the babies that had been orphaned. I rang after a few weeks. The gestation period is only 21 days, and he said the babies had been born, but unfortunately Mamma had eaten them all the next day! The other female had not had any at all. We were not happy about Paddy, who was still very wild and wouldn't tolerate handling. The day of the move I rang Mr Lawson, who said he would change Paddy for us and have another coloured mate ready. We came home in the end with a beautiful gold and white male we called Muffin, and a pale

sandy gold-and-white female we called Nipper, after she had caught
Tessa's finger one day. I had visions of starting a new dynasty of unusual
hamsters in Mombasa, which, regrettably, was doomed to failure. They
were a charming pair, very tame, and we loved them very much. A few
weeks after the move we put them together, and waited with baited
breath (I thought it would be a good practical demonstration to the
children on the Facts of Life). Evidently we had not hit the right day as
she spurned his advances and tried to bite him. Mr Lawson's little book
told us that impotence could result if a male was really rebuffed and
bitten, so we hurriedly removed our 'stud' and tried again next day.
Still it wasn't the opportune moment, and it was a case of 'third time
lucky'. The marriage was consummated under the stares of three pairs
of fascinated eyes (Leslie refused to watch and said it wasn't decent to
spy on them). Three weeks later – nothing. Undaunted, we tried again,
with the same result. A third attempt did seem, after the second week,
to have caused a bulge in Nipper's tummy. Sure enough, she later had
four minute pink, naked babies, but like Tabitha Twitchet, she was an
anxious parent and kept moving the nest about the cage and shedding
babies all over the place. Two were dead by the first day, and the other
two died next day. She had not harmed them deliberately, because I
could find no marks on the pathetic little pink corpses. Perhaps the
strain of constantly being carried about from one place to another was
too much for them. Anyhow, our only excursion into hamster breeding
ended disastrously. A week later Nipper herself got ill and died and
poor Muffin was left a widow. It is very hard to find anyone who
knows about these little animals. I did write to Mr Lawson after the
death of the babies, but I muddled the address, I think, because I never
had a reply and I was too discouraged to write again when, some
months later, Muffin went off his food and died within a few days. I
wondered if the hotter climate might be responsible; it was a great
contrast to Nairobi.

As ever, I've digressed, so we must go back to that chaotic Friday of
the move. A huge moving van arrived early, with several men carrying
vast rolls of polythene, tea-chests of packing materials and miles of
brown paper. I had decided that Tigga must be shut up all day. I know
cats hate a change and I could just see her taking off and vanishing
into thin air at the wrong moment. Joan Morley next door offered to
have us for a sandwich lunch, which was a great help, and it seemed a

very long time later that we sat on her veranda in the afternoon having a last cup of tea before finally leaving for the hotel. I had conned the manager of this establishment ('No pets allowed in the hotel') into having our menagerie for just one night, and the two hamster cages sat on the table in one room with Tigga prowling ominously about, howling dolefully at intervals. I had to leave the windows open only a crack or she would have been off. We spent a slightly restless night. The children in the adjoining room were very excited and there was something, apparently in football boots, galloping about in the roof above.

We had asked for an early breakfast at 6.00 a.m., and we were positively awed at the result. Spot on time, a steward carried in two trays. There was a pot of tea, a pot of coffee, a plate of cheese sand-wiches and a plate of brilliant yellow Madeira cake. After recovering from the shock, we all tucked in, including most of the livestock. We loaded up the car and by 7.15 we were off. In the back were Neal, Sarah and Tessa, with Ping squeezed in as well. Tigga was vociferous in her box in the boot; we had the Renault 16 and you can take out the back window shelf and get to the boot, so she was quite all right and was let out at intervals. In the front I had the hamster cages by my feet and Skip beside me. You can imagine the face of the policeman who stopped us at a checkpoint at Voi. He peered in and was fascinated at Tigga jostling among the dogs, squinting with emotion and making her Siamese cries. He asked if they all got on well, and thought it was a good joke. I don't think he'd ever seen cats and dogs together like that.

We passed some elephants on the road and stopped to look at them. Pingle was very bossy, and barked out of the window at them. We think she must be the only Ceylonese pi-dog to bark at wild African elephants!

At midday, we reached Mombasa. The town part is actually an island and is reached from Nairobi on the north side by going over the Makupa Causeway and emerging on the other side via Nyali Bridge. There is also a ferry which takes you to Likoni on the south coast. We got to our bungalow and spotted the removal van parked under a tree. The driver told us that the men to do the actual carrying had not yet arrived. (We found later they were still in town, shifting all the office furniture and equipment, which of course had to come too, into our smart new office in Kilindini Road.)

It was a beautiful day and we sat under a tree and ate the picnic lunch we had brought. Still no removal men appeared, so the driver and his mate decided to make a start. We were having the house painted and one of the painters was co-opted into helping, and in the end we got straight. After a series of phone calls, the rest of the men turned up at about five o'clock and finished the job. It looked most odd to see our Nairobi furniture in different surroundings and I hated the gap on the television table . . .

Everyone had told us how friendly people were in Mombasa, and certainly we settled down rapidly. The girls started school at Mombasa Primary and did well, and they made new friends of all races in a very short time.

Leslie decided to buy a boat and when an aunt died and left him some money, he bought a 14 ft. fibre-glass Dory with a 50 h.p. Mercury engine, and we christened her (with tea, of course) 'Auntie Flo', in memory of her founder. I swopped some old riding breeches of Sarah's for a pair of water skis with a friend, and we had some hectic sessions learning how to use them. The children got the knack very quickly and, to my disgust, Leslie stood up on his third attempt. Unfortunately he suffers from a personality change as soon as he gets his hands on that expensive handle with the nylon rope on it. I find it extremely difficult to steer the boat, maintain the right speed, look out for swimmers under my bows, and interpret Leslie's infuriated gestures with one hand, as I crane painfully over my shoulder. My mind gels, I panic, I *know*, in any case, that whatever I do is bound to be wrong. My intrepid skier waves, roars, shakes his head and glares, and finally sinks in a welter of malevolent bubbles. 'Too *slow*', he howls as he surfaces. 'Now, for heaven's sake, go the way I show,' and off we go again. How I hated those first few sessions, and to make things worse, I found I couldn't even get up on the damn things. My arms felt as if they had been ripped out of their sockets after only a few tries, and I was bruised on the shins from the skis. Then we got a large wooden disc, which you lie on – much easier, except when Leslie went too fast, without bothering to watch me, just what he told *me* not to do when I was driving! Down went the disc with me fighting to keep my head above the water, yelling abuse at L., and afterwards he said I sounded just like him. After that I gave up water-skiing. I did once manage to 'get up' for a few hectic seconds, and that was quite enough for me.

The bungalow, Nyali, Mombasa, 1968.

One day in December we were cruising *Auntie Flo* round Kilindini Harbour. We wanted to see a Greek ship that had invited us to a party next day. We found her and as we came closer, noticed several of her crew leaning over the side waving gaily. Thinking my shorts were responsible for this demonstration of enthusiasm, I preened myself but then saw that they were, in fact, watching a small object swimming frantically alongside the ship. A simultaneous shriek went up from me and the children: 'Daddy, quick, *save* it!' With a groan from Leslie, we altered course. I lent perilously over the side and with much struggling and squawking, fished out our intrepid swimmer – a sodden, barely recognisable cock! The crew cheered as we wrapped him in Sarah's jersey, and they waved to indicate we could keep our shipwrecked mariner. We were most intrigued to know his story, but as with so many of our pets, never found out how long he had been swimming or how he fell in. When we went aboard the *Hellenic Glory*, we asked the Captain if he had missed out on a chicken curry the day before, but he said they never had any livestock aboard. Anyhow, once he was dried out, he turned out to be a very handsome bird, brown and white speckled, with a loud voice. We called him Robinson Coucou (the latter is Swahili for chicken) and he lived in the garden tethered by one leg with a long piece of string. I didn't like this very much and after we had had him a few weeks, I let him loose, but he wandered too much and I was scared he'd end up in someone's pot. One day he slipped his tether and I spent a frustrating time chasing him; I was only in a swimsuit as I'd been sunbathing when I heard his triumphant crow coming from somewhere it had no business to be. Tessa and I tried to corner him but he was too cunning. He flew over our heads and ran off. *How* he ran, crouched low like a pheasant, his legs a positive blur. We pelted after but he vanished into thin air. We discovered his trick was to swerve suddenly and crouch low in a bunch of long grass. Hot and furious, I abandoned the chase and listened to his triumphant crow receding into the distance. Joas, the gardener, joined in the hunt, but by teatime we all went out to have a swim in a friend's pool. When we got back, it was after dark and there was Joas, just returning Robinson to his house. He was minus all his tail feathers, so had led someone a dance; I couldn't gather from Joas the full story. My Swahili is not too fluent but the police were mentioned and I was rather touched that Joas should bother to catch a silly bird which he thought would doubtless be better on the table for Christmas. About a month ago Robinson went to a new home. For some time I'd felt a bit sorry for him all alone, and he'd had a narrow escape three times, when he'd gone up a tree to roost, got tangled with his string, and ended up hanging head down by one leg, poor chap. Leslie's secretary, Jackie, told me she had a hen, which had been given her to eat and had survived unscathed as Jackie was soft-hearted. The hen had had an affair with a neighbouring cock and now had a small family of chicks. She offered to have Robinson, and we accepted, knowing he would be far happier there. We had a hilarious time watching him chase his reluctant bride all over Jackie's garden, but it was his fault; he was far too pushing and lacked finesse in his approach. Jackie told us next day that the first husband had come over to inspect his new rival and there had been a fight. The intruder had been driven off by the gardener, but had cunningly returned next day with a friend, and between them roughed up poor Robinson a bit before help came. He was fearfully pleased with himself, Jackie said, and bloody but unbowed, crowed like mad. After that he had no more trouble, and I hear his wife is broody again so we hope she has some handsome speckled babies soon. We miss his early morning crow and I sometimes wonder if Tigga has noticed his absence. When we first had Robinson, I was worried that Tigga might have designs on his person and I kept an eye on her. She was absolutely fascinated by him and used to lie for hours watching him from a few feet away. I discovered I need not worry about his safety; he kept her firmly in place. If she sneaked up too close, he would droop his wings threateningly, making ominous noises and sidling up to her. Once when she tried to squeeze past him and a wall, he gave her a whack with his wing and a swipe with his beak and she fled. I had a feeling she never quite made up her mind exactly what he was. A bird, to her, was something small and agile, which (to our rage) she occasionally managed to catch, though not often. It certainly bore little resemblance to this large and loud-voiced creature who was actually able to retaliate if she tried any funny business. She brooded darkly about this, lurking behind bushes or plants watching Robinson. On the odd occasion when she did stalk him and even charge, she was always put off by his flapping leap in the air and would slink away, foiled again, while Robinson retrieved his dignity, looking more pompous than ever. I used to get a lot of fun from watching these encounters. It really needed a movie film to record the drama.

It was early in December when we acquired one of the most fascinating pets we have ever had. Sarah came home from school with a small, rather dull-looking fledgling which I recognised as a Mousebird. These are very common in Kenya and swoop from tree to tree in large flocks, chattering and chirruping as they creep about the branches looking for insects and also eating off tender buds and shoots. This and their taste for soft fruit make them the farmer's sworn enemy, but after six months close contact with these charming little birds, I feel the world should be told; they make the finest pets in bird-dom! For sheer kooky entertainment, they are the tops. What other bird hangs like a bat by its feet from the roof, can turn its head through 180 degrees like an owl, climbs like a woodpecker, sunbathes like a penguin, dustbathes like a chicken, has a crest like a skylark, and has such odd feet and toes, he has to be placed by baffled naturalists in his own Order, called Coliiformes? It seems that the large red feet of the mouse-bird are exceptional in that the toes can be arranged either three front and one back, like most birds, or two front and two back, like parrots and woodpeckers. Certainly, they use their feet like a parrot to hold food as they peck at it with their strong finch-like beaks. At

Lesley Holland having her hair done by Mousie, Mombasa, 1969.

first glance, you might think my wonder bird is a bit dowdy. About blue-tit size about the body, Mousebirds have a very long tail, which must account for about eight or nine inches of their total length. The top part of the body and wings is dark brown, the chest russet, lightly barred under the throat. Cheeks have a white patch and there is a bare circle of grey skin round each eye that gives a slightly debauched look to the bird. The total effect is topped of by a jaunty crest, which, for some reason of mouse-bird etiquette, is always lowered when eating. When they drink, you will not be surprised to know that they do not sip like most birds, but take a long pull, rather like a pigeon. To top it all, what other bird enjoys a bath on wet lettuce and tries to take a dustbath on your lap?

When Sarah's friend Robin found Mousie, he was in a bush and was far from being a helpless fledgling. I have looked up all I can about the species, and the books say the babies leave the nest when they are nearly fledged and creep about the branches in search of food, returning home at night. Later, they join the flock and are fed by anyone who happens to feel like it, and live in a happy communal atmosphere for the rest of their lives. When I saw Mousie sitting placidly in his box, I thought we had our usual 'five-day fledgling', for in the past we have tried to rear so many pathetic orphans, which died a few days later. Sarah said he ate pawpaw and by gosh, he did! Fluttering his wings in supplication, he waded through vast quantities of the fruit, which then seemed to emerge the other end unchanged. I felt this wasn't right so I made up a sort of mash, adding rolled oats or Farex to the fruit, and things improved. About a month after we got him, I woke up to the fact that Mousie was here to stay and that he needed a far more permanent home than the old hamster cage he lived in when he wasn't riding about clinging to the front of someone's shirt. I was very lucky to find a friend who had a large budgie breeding cage that was not needed and Mousie settled in happily, though he much preferred to be out and about exploring. He adores the dogs, flying down to them on the floor, nibbling at their nails, and, regrettably, at Pingles nipples, poor dear! They are very patient with him. They usually get up and walk away after a moment, and we see that he doesn't make too much of a pest of himself. Sometimes he takes a ride on their back and he revels in Skipper's long tail, snuggling into it and nibbling at the long strands. He has a bit of a hair fetish, and likes long human hair too, preferably wet after a bath. I read that they enjoyed dust baths and was delighted when he instantly went through the motions when I put him in a dusty patch. He fluffed and bowed and scuffled, just as my hens used to do, sneezing occasionally and staying in far too long. He was easy to feed. One book said they sometimes took nestlings (horror! Not *our* Mousie, surely?) so I offered him raw minced beef and it went down with a disgraceful exhibition of greed. In the course of his career he has enjoyed iced coffee, tea (sucked up from the spoon with astonishing speed) jelly-babies and orange squash, apart from soft fruits, raisins, lettuce and rolled oats. We had read about the very highly developed social life of mousebirds and hoped he wasn't lonely. A mirror in his cage helped, and he spent a lot of time ogling himself, but I did feel we ought perhaps to let him go. I took him out in the garden several times, timing my visits to coincide with flocks of wild mousies. He peered vaguely in their direction but didn't seem to recognise them. I put him into bushes and trees and he enjoyed exploring, but always came back to me after a few minutes. I was touched, but still not entirely happy. I don't like wild birds to be caged. Then, about a month after we got him, Tessa trod on him by mistake and broke his leg just above the joint, in an impossible place for all the match sticks that everyone wisely recommended. We suddenly noticed that his right leg was sticking out at right angles to his body and seemed limp and useless. He seemed cheerful enough, and more irritated by it than anything else. I managed to put a piece of insulating tape over the joint to try and immobilise it. It wasn't very successful and he kept nibbling at it, so after a week I took it off. Gradually, the leg went back into place and grew stronger, and three weeks later was as good as new! He never even went off his feed or showed any signs of pain, but looked pathetic with it hanging useless, it got in the way so. We thought this was a good indication of the toughness of these quaint little birds, but about two months after his accident an incredible coincidence showed he was not just a random example of Coliiformes resilience. We were driving past the house where Sarah's friend Robin had found Mousie and we saw Robin outside with something in his hand. We stopped to say hello, and Robin said 'I was just coming round to you; I've got another mousie here,' and handed me the most miserable little object I'd seen for a long time. She had no tail whatsoever, which was bad enough, but then I found half her wing gone and a tiny blob of blood at the end of the bone showing that the terminal bone of the wing had been bitten(?) clean off. She was in shock, eyes closed, feathers ruffled, though she struggled feebly at first. With very mixed feelings, and promising to let Robin know how she fared, we took her home. I put her in a hamster cage on her own. At first we thought the companionship of her own species might help her, but when we put her in Mousie's cage, he was so pushing in his attentions we thought he would do more harm than good and took her out. Mousie couldn't believe that the cold mirror-bird had at last come to life, and he craned his neck incredulously, going all thin with excitement and hopping down to look closer. But then he began to tweak at her feathers and jostle her about, and we weren't at all sure of his motives so we took her out. I ought to explain here that though we always called Mousie 'he', mousebird sex is a dark secret, known only to another mousebird, and it was purely wishful thinking that made us call the newcomer 'she' and later, Minnie, or Mrs Mousie. We never honestly thought she would live, but next day she seemed a little better, so we put her back with Mousie and watched, fascinated, at the way he greeted her, tweaked out a few feathers, stamped on her with a large red foot, and held long twittering conversations. Crests went up and down like yo-yos, and when she hopped up onto a low perch, we were thrilled. All day we kept an eye on them, and though Mousie seemed a bit rough, she gave the impression of being happy and began to eat and drink. It was a wonderful shock to us all when it became quite clear that she was going to live. New feathers grew, and now, two and a half months later, she has a longer tail than Mousie. The wing feathers have also grown, and one can hardly notice that they are shorter on one side than the other. She has never become as tame as Mousie, but will come to the bars and snatch food from my fingers, but that is as far as she will trust us. She calls loudly to Mousie if he is taken out, and I think we are right about their sex; he does sometimes offer her bits of food, though mostly he rudely gulps it down and ignores her. Their lettuce baths I saw by accident one day. I had put in some lettuce for them, fastened by the ingenious maker of the cage by means of a bulldog-clip screwed to the door. The lettuce had seemed a bit tired, so I dunked it under the tap and clipped it in. Mousie immediately flew down to it, sat right on top and proceeded to rub his chin in it, rather as Tigga does. Then he started going through bath-like motions with his wings, scuffling about with great glee! Minnie tried to join him but found it rather difficult; he would hog the whole thing and they got very mixed up. Both finally emerged, satisfyingly wet, so that even Minnie's crest looked damp and sticky. All the time they made twitterings and squawkings to each other, a sort of running commentary. I stood by open-mouthed, giggling like an idiot and wishing the rest of the family were there to see. Later on they did repeat this idiocy for a bigger audience, but it struck me as odd that they preferred it like this to taking a shallow bath in their water-bowl. They have given us such pleasure, these kinky creatures, and at night they either hang from the roof like peculiar bats, or snuggle up side by side, clinging vertically onto the bars. Nothing so ordinary as a perch for a mousebird! I hope one day that Gerald Durrel will acquire one; he could really do justice to them in his books.

Mousie's exploits bring my story to an end. I have been wondering for some weeks exactly how to finish this book. Many animal books have an ending that wrings your heart, and I am left moist-eyed and lump-in-throat. However, there is enough sadness in this world, so I'm glad to end on a happy note. Skipper lies near me, nose on paws, digesting a substantial lunch; Ping is curled up on the rug, also asleep, and the mousies are doubtless up to some antic, swinging about the ceiling like orang-utangs. Two things, said by people in very different circumstances and places, seem to me to be relevant here.

The first was at the last Shaggy Dog Show. Skipper was in the ring with Neal and I heard one lady who was standing behind me say to her friend, 'That little dog must be very much loved.' I have never forgotten that remark. I am proud to think Skipper was able to convey to an outsider how much she means to us all in the family.

The second remark was made by a Norwegian neighbour of mine, whose elderly husband died with tragic suddenness on Christmas night. She called us in to help and it was much later, as she sat numbly on our sofa sipping brandy, that she asked me if I had a family, for we did not know her at all, nor she us. I told her about the children and I have never forgotten her simple answer. 'You are very much blessed,' she said.

This just about serves as my ending. I am indeed very much blessed. I have my loving husband, fine children, many friends, a lovely home, and my faithful pets. If I have amused or diverted any of my readers and helped them to forget their troubles for a few hours, then I am well satisfied.

Mombasa
1969

CHAPTER 21

Thirty-one years later

AFTER FINISHING THIS BOOK IN 1969, I sent it hopefully to Curtis Browne, the London literary agents. They politely declined to take it so *Travels of a Tea-Taster's Dog* lay around in trunks and drawers, and latterly on a footstool in the sitting room, occasionally dipped into by one of the family. I had also sent the first few chapters to Michaela Denis, who lived in Nairobi and whom I knew by sight. She wrote back saying that it was a difficult market to get into and that *Born Free* had been turned down by six publishers before being finally accepted. I gave up my literary ambitions until, with the Millennium and my 70th birthday looming, I began to explore the possibility of publishing my letters. These, written between 1955 and 1966, were to my parents. Over the years we have found hours of nostalgic fun in reading them aloud. However, the letters were in longhand for the most part and would need a deal of sorting, editing and typing – not an easy proposition. Then suddenly I realised that I had a complete manuscript ready typed in a file, just waiting to be unleashed on an unsuspecting public. So here it is!

Of course in the last thirty-one years much has happened. A few months after I'd finished the book, Skipper died. We had been on leave and Stan and Margaret Holland were living in the bungalow, looking after Skip, Ping and the cats. Margaret, with Lesley, went back to the U.K. a little early and it fell to Stan to nurse the ailing 14-year-old Skip, who finally died only five days before our return. Poor Stan – he was very upset! We felt for him deeply. He had loved Skip and he had a little coffin made and buried her in the garden.

In 1976 we returned home to the U.K. for good. Lipton's London Office was moving down to Walton-on-Thames and poor Leslie endured three months of commuting in the Great Hot Summer. He survived that and a move to Weybridge. The children grew up and left home (not too far away) and in 1981 we moved to Puttenham. In 1985 Leslie went back to Mombasa, supposedly for four months, while

Sarah, Neal and Tess, Puttenham, 2000, our 45th wedding anniversary.

Gilbert went on leave. I was due to follow ten days later. On his first night back in our old bungalow, Leslie had a coronary and was taken into Intensive Care. I went out to join him and we spent five weeks lazing about in luxury hotels, so that by the time we got back to the U.K. he was looking pretty fit. However, the specialist said he must take early retirement, which he did. The occasion was marked with a splendid office party and a 'This Is Your Life' with gifts from all the different places in which we had lived.

So the past fifteen years have been involved with village business: bell-ringing, Meals on Wheels etc., as well as enjoying our family. We have four grandchildren, aged from six to ten years old. We have had three dogs since Skip and Ping. The last-named had to be put to sleep in '73, at the age of fourteen. Then in '69 we got Tara, a black Schnauzer, and after her came Pickle, a rescue mongrel. Finally in '96 Buster came and took us over. In temperament and character he is close to Skip, friendly, quiet – a real lap-dog. He and I do 'Pets As Therapy' visits to our local hospice, nursing home and Day Centres. All our dogs have been part of the family, much loved and mourned on their deaths, but Skipper has a special place in our lives. She shared so much with us,

We look back on our days Out There with great pleasure and nostalgia. When I watch travel programmes, I find myself quite emotional. The bird song especially takes me back: the clear warble of a bulbul means the cool of early morning in a Ceylon nursing home; the 'tonk, tonk, tonk' of the Coppersmith in India, the monotonous 'koel, koel, koel' of the aptly-named cuckoo called the Koel, the purr of the mourning dove in the Game Parks of Kenya – all these bring back fond memories, which I'm very happy to have shared with you.

Puttenham
May, 2000